NATURAL FACILITATORS

A Key to Successful Organizations

KIM MARVEL, PH.D.

Natural Facilitators: A Key to Successful Organizations
Published by RGH Press
1357 Northern Court, Fort Collins, CO 80521

Cover and interior design by Launie Parry, Red Letter Creative
Edited by Karla Oceanak

ISBN: 978-0-578-70955-0

1. Business/leadership 2. Organization 3. Management

Printed in the United States of America
First Edition 2020

Contents

PART ONE: OVERVIEW AND METHODS

Introduction

All eyes were on me. There I was, sitting at a small table with three others in a nondescript hospital meeting room. As director of the Organizational Development department, I had finished my presentation. After a lengthy pause in the conversation, the next move was mine. This was the second meeting on the same topic with the same people; we were at an impasse.

Across the table, the two men from the Information Technology (IT) department opposed my proposal. Sitting on my right was Lindsey, my talented but very frustrated educational technologist.

> "If you can't explain it simply, you don't understand it well enough."
>
> ALBERT EINSTEIN

At stake was the method of delivering the annual mandatory training required of all hospital employees—uninteresting but important topics such as fire safety and handling hazardous materials. The current online training method was lengthy, tedious, and inefficient—dry, text-heavy teaching modules followed by endless multiple-choice questions. I had received an earful of employee complaints about it. The department I led was responsible for the quality of the training, and I felt intense pressure to improve it. The good news was that Lindsey and I had found a solution that had been implemented successfully in other hospital systems:

a software program that allowed for interactive learning using avatars and real-life scenarios. We were both excited about the prospect of this break-through, and Lindsey was prepared to develop the innovative modules. All we needed was the new software.

I glanced again across the table, where the director and middle manager from IT sat silently. Moments before, they had explained why the new software could not be purchased. With grim smiles, they reiterated their reasons: budget limitations...it might overload the server...the IT department must test the software before it can be approved...they currently were backlogged. Though Lindsey and I had presented our rationale for the last thirty minutes, they hadn't budged. From my perspective, they saw Lindsey and me as a threat to their control over hospital software. In the momentary silence, the plastic chairs became even more uncomfortable. The overhead lights buzzed faintly. I pondered my next move.

The situation cried out for assertive leadership from me. I could have acknowledged our impasse and informed them of my decision to escalate the issue up to the next level of senior hospital leadership—a strategy to overcome the stalemate. Instead, I fell back on my natural tendency to search for a consensus—a plan both sides could agree on. I urged them to reconsider the needed software, and we disbanded. Lindsey left the meeting disappointed and frustrated.

The new software was never purchased. The ineffective training method remained in place.

I'm embarrassed to tell you about that meeting because it feels like I failed as leader. However, it was the inflection point at which I became aware that my natural tendencies were impeding my ability to lead the department. You see, I strongly prefer to help groups come up with solutions together, to find consensus. I'm less comfortable and skilled asserting my opinion to influence others, especially in situations with strong emotions or opposition. In the meeting, my desire to facilitate a discussion, maintain positive relationships, and have the group come to an agreement was stronger than my desire to push my agenda, which, in retrospect, would have been the better choice.

I'm a facilitator by nature but also by nurture. I was trained as a clinical psychologist, which helped prepare me to create a trusting atmosphere in which others could speak openly, without fear of judgment. In the early years of my career, my facilitation skills were a good fit with my work roles. Over time I was promoted into management and leadership positions in healthcare—first in medical education, training family doctors and counseling medical patients with mental health concerns, then directing the organizational development department in a two-hospital system, and eventually directing a network of family medicine residency programs.

After that failed meeting, I continued in leadership positions for several more years. But I became increasingly aware of the gaps between the expectations of a leader and my natural strengths and preferences as a facilitator. The typical descriptions of leadership in bestselling business books didn't fit me. I read about characteristics of effective leaders: influence, vision, inspiration, decision-making, communication, and providing resources. Yet despite my career progression into formal leadership positions, I was most content and effective when organizing projects and events, assisting others to make decisions, helping people get along with each other, and smoothing out internal processes. In short, there were many times when my natural inclinations to facilitate undermined my ability to lead.

My growing awareness of the differences between facilitation and leadership roles led to important questions. Effective leaders use a variety of approaches to influence others and the direction of the organization. But what about the people who care deeply about an organization and its mission yet don't desire to shape the strategic plan or be in a highly influential role? What do we know about the people "behind the scenes" who are skilled at organizing and accomplishing projects and tasks delegated to them by leaders? Are these people more satisfied and effective when they remain in facilitation roles rather than moving into management or leadership roles, as I had done?

This book is about the talented people in organizations, teams, and families who are not leaders but who help get things done. They enable others to do their own jobs better. They support the decision-makers. They are the facilitators. The trouble is that their contributions and skill set are not always noticed or celebrated. Indeed, their value may only be recognized in retrospect, after they leave an organization and productivity or morale decline. By better understanding the value of facilitators, leaders and managers can hire and place these special people in ways that benefit their organizations. And those who identify as facilitators can feel validated about their important role and be thoughtful about the career choices they make.

Let's look at a few examples to see how people with all kinds of backgrounds facilitate in diverse settings. These examples help illustrate the behaviors that may slip by unnoticed to the untrained eye.

SHANE

Shane Battier played professional basketball in the National Basketball Association for many years. He was not an all-star. He did not score many points, block many shots, or grab many rebounds. But when he was on the court, his team had a higher winning percentage. His high school coach commented, "He has this incredible ability to make everyone around him better." Writer Michael Lewis[1] states that Battier's contributions were subtle and hard-to-measure. When sports analysts scrutinized videotapes, it was apparent that Battier positioned himself so his teammates could get more rebounds. His coaches assigned him to defend the best offensive player on the opposing team. While Battier may have had good instincts, he heightened them with research. He prepared in advance, spending hours preparing for games by studying statistics and predominant moves of the opponent. Even though he played a secondary role, when Battier was on the court he enabled those around him to perform better. His contributions would be easy to overlook, with the focus instead on the high-scoring all-stars. However, from a team perspective, his subtle contributions made all the difference.

FRAN

Extended families are complex systems. In many ways they are similar to organizations. Members typically have differing values, varied communication preferences, and a wide range of social comfort during gatherings. My mother, Fran Marvel, was a skilled facilitator for our extended family. When she was around, people seemed more at ease, conversations were relaxed and inclusive of all members, and people expressed their satisfaction when the gathering ended. However, her contributions were quite subtle, requiring close observation. It was clear that family members enjoyed her presence. But what specific actions made the gatherings go more smoothly?

I can picture Mom at a family reunion in my parents' cabin. As this gathering started, some of us were standing and others sitting in folding chairs scattered around the living room. My adult cousins, who had traveled from their distant rural homes, seemed particularly uncomfortable in the social setting. They sat silently, watching as others chatted informally.

I sat and watched Mom from across the room. In her older years she was short in stature but moved easily among others. She approached my cousins with her friendly and welcoming manner. Gentle and warmhearted, she greeted them personally with a smile, eye contact, and a hug. She reached out to touch them, sometimes holding a hand, as she talked. Her caring and compassion were obvious. We all felt valued. A less obvious skill was her ability to facilitate conversations. She invited others in. As she moved around the room, she sometimes led isolated individuals closer to other family members to start a new conversation. Her questions showed an awareness of the others' interests and experience—an ability to step into someone else's world. This was particularly valuable for those relatives who lacked self-confidence in social situations. Her comments and reflections encouraged others to open up and share their thoughts. Her personalized comments showed that she cared about others, valuing them by remembering specific details about their lives. Social discomfort was further reduced by her subtle wit. She was not one to tell jokes or narrate elaborate stories. Rather, she lightened ongoing conversations by inserting humorous phrases or setting up another family member to share a funny experience. People smiled and laughed more when she was involved. After conversing with several relatives, she slipped out of the room momentarily. She re-emerged with a tray of snacks and passed refreshments between sub-groups. She made sure everyone had a comfortable chair. In addition to facilitating social interaction, she recognized the value of other ingredients for a successful social gathering. Again, these were subtle but helpful additions. Her sensitivity to the needs of others was exceptional. It is noteworthy that her husband, my father, was a successful leader. Undoubtedly, my mother, with her ability to facilitate, played a significant role in my father's career success. Mom passed away several years ago. My family continues to miss her warmth and her soft-spoken ability to bring people closer together with her presence.

CINDY

The next example of facilitating comes from a coworker I will refer to as Cindy. Members of our small hospital department volunteered at the local food bank twice a year. Our few hours helping out in the storage facility provided a community service and strengthened our team. On one occasion, seven of us were given the task of organizing donated canned goods. Jumbled cans were heaped in two large bins. Our job was to sort food by types. For example, we were to pick out the cans of chili and walk them over to a box labelled "chili," find the cans of soup and place them in the "soup" box, and so on. We eagerly dived in, each picking through the piles of cans to find similar foods and, after several minutes of searching, taking an armful of cans to the appropriate box. As we were carrying on, conversing amiably and searching through the piles, I noticed that Cindy started doing something different. She remained by one of the large bins, rotating the cans so the labels faced the front. She no longer dug through the pile; she instead made the labels more visible for others. This simple change allowed everyone else to become much more efficient. Initially, no one noticed what she was doing. Then she was gently chided by a colleague for not working as hard as everyone else. But eventually, as she rotated all the cans in the two large bins, everyone continued with the more efficient process. No one commented about her creative thinking, her facilitation, and how it made others more productive, but I made a mental note and tucked this example away to share with you now. This woman was doing exactly what I hope to describe to you in more detail in the following chapters.

KIM

My own work experience underscores the value of facilitating and the importance of understanding one's role in an organization. I am my own fourth example. As the executive director of a statewide network of non-profit organizations, I initially viewed my position through the lens of traditional leadership models. However, over time, I saw my natural strength and preference was carrying out the decisions of others. I spent considerable time planning meetings and events, soliciting opinions of leaders, and attending to details. As I revealed at the opening of the introduction, some of my innate tendencies interfered with traditional leadership responsibilities. My sensitivity to others' emotions was stressful, and my natural preference to accommodate all opinions inhibited assertive decision-making, including managing my staff. I found it more satisfying to organize processes, facilitate meetings, and document progress than to take part in free-flowing group discussions to generate new strategies. I was better suited to carry out a vision rather than create one. Upon self-reflection, reading, and discussions with trusted colleagues, I began to view my skills and natural inclinations as enabling others and facilitating processes rather than leading and influencing others. Acknowledging this tendency helped me embrace my areas of strength and use them to benefit the organization.

By personal experience and observation of others, I have come to recognize and appreciate facilitation as a skill set that is often overlooked. When processes are going "smoothly" or projects are progressing in a system, organization, or family, there is likely a skilled facilitator involved. Most of these people are *natural* facilitators—they are not trained to be facilitators; it just seems to be a part of their DNA.

I have shared this concept with professional colleagues and family members. Many recognized the facilitating role in their own area of work. A physician pointed to "practice coaches" employed in medical clinics to improve work flow. One colleague in higher education talked about department vice-chairs or administrative assistants, who often fill the facilitator role. Typically, the leaders were described as visionaries focused on the big picture or creating an ideal future, or as overworked individuals burdened with budgetary and political battles. They needed someone, a natural facilitator, to keep them organized and follow through on details. Another colleague, upon hearing about this concept of facilitation, told me of a large healthcare system that established a full-time position to float among departments, understand their interconnections, and coordinate process changes. The role, he said, resulted in a more efficient system.

In my initial discussions, this concept resonated with people of various backgrounds even if they used different terminology to describe the facilitator role. The commonality was enabling others to perform better. These people facilitated processes, literally "making things easier" for others. To better understand natural facilitators, three years ago I interviewed several employees and their supervisors in four medical clinics. After the pilot project was completed,[2] I decided to expand my research by interviewing a larger number of employees and supervisors in a variety of organizations. The results of the interviews, presented in this book, show that natural facilitators can be found in all types of organizations. They help other people to be more productive and ensure that processes flow more smoothly. Also, I discovered that the personal attributes of natural facilitators differ from those of leaders and managers. All three roles—leader, manager, and facilitator—are complementary and play a distinct part in successful organizations.

If you are a leader or manager, my hope is that you will use this book to recognize the value of natural facilitators. Leaders, this information will help you place natural facilitators where they will be most beneficial to the organization. Managers, you can consider the characteristics of natural facilitators when screening job applicants and celebrating the strengths of current employees. Although this book is written primarily for leaders and managers, natural facilitators may find it helpful to apply the findings to make thoughtful career decisions and enhance their work satisfaction. To the natural facilitators reading this book, you will likely find yourself nodding in agreement with the characteristics presented in chapters 3-10. The discussion about challenges (chapter 11) and the suggestions for preparing for leadership and management (chapter 12) will be especially helpful.

In the following two chapters, I define facilitation and explain why natural facilitators are valuable to organizations. And, for those interested in the interviews and participants, I provide more details about the people I talked to and where they work. This will set the stage for the second section, in which I present the specific characteristics of natural facilitators.

Overview and Methods

CHAPTER 1

Facilitation
Why It's Important

In a later section I describe the characteristics of facilitators identified through my research. But before we begin, let's first define terms and clarify why a more complete understanding of facilitation is valuable.

"Facilitate: To make easy or easier."

THE AMERICAN HERITAGE COLLEGE DICTIONARY

DEFINITIONS

The verb "facilitate" means to make a process or action easier.[3] Synonyms include ease, grease, loosen up, smooth, and unclog. In the context of the present study, a facilitator is a person who makes processes easier for others. The behavior of this person helps "to make things go smoother" or "to make things go more easily."

Before settling on the term *facilitator* for this book, I also considered *enabler* and *human catalyst*. The verb "enable" means to make possible, practical, or easy. Using that definition, the *enabler* role can be desirable for organizations, including families. However, in recent decades, the term *enabler* has emerged in the field of addiction studies to describe a person who gives misguided support for someone with a substance-abuse issue. In that case, an enabler inadvertently supports the self-destructive behavior of another. Because of its negative connotation, I have avoided the term *enabler*.

I also considered the term *human catalyst*—a person who facilitates or mediates a human "chemical reaction" or system process without themselves being consumed in the reaction.[4] In the field of chemistry, a catalyst is a substance that increases the rate of a chemical reaction but is not consumed in the process. Likewise, a human can be a catalyst for team projects by helping tasks get completed and people work together more efficiently. However, as defined, a human catalyst is separate from the people who complete the work. The human catalyst is added to stimulate change but not do the work itself. Because my interest is people who are part of the day-to-day workforce and often complete the work, not those in a designated role to bring about change, I ultimately decided to use the term *facilitator*.

The term *facilitator* also has limitations, however. It is commonly used too narrowly to describe a person skilled at leading discussions or meetings. Such a specific definition does not capture the breadth of the term. Facilitate comes from the term "facile," which means easily accomplished or attained. Facilitating, as described in this book, includes a wide range of behaviors that make things "go more easily" for others. It includes, but is not limited to, leading discussions.

Ultimately, I added the term *natural* to emphasize these people are not trained facilitators. Their facilitation skills are inborn or learned at a young age. They bring their facilitation skills with them into their formal job responsibilities.

Finally, the term *exemplary* warrants comment. Exemplary means "worthy of imitation; commendable; serving as a model." It is used to emphasize the goal of the study: to understand those individuals who are the best at facilitating processes. During my discussions with organizational leaders and family members, it became evident that many people can offer at least limited assistance with processes. Most of us have some facilitation skills. But to truly understand the core attributes of facilitators, it was necessary to seek out exemplars: those individuals identified as excelling in this role.

THE POWER OF METAPHORS

When describing the concept of an exemplary facilitator, I have found metaphors to be a useful tool. For example, facilitators are good at *greasing the wheels*. In a literal sense, this action is done by a car mechanic by inserting grease into the moving parts of a wheel. The grease helps the wheel turn more smoothly by reducing friction, thereby avoiding overheating and the premature wearing down of metal parts. In a figurative sense, a facilitator reduces friction by planning ahead, preparing materials, reducing stress among people (thereby avoiding emotional overheating), and making the process run more smoothly. The work of a mechanic is done under the hood or the undercarriage of a car, out of sight of most drivers. The driver may not be aware that greasing has been completed, so long as the wheels run smoothly. Similarly, a facilitator's work may go unnoticed by leaders and managers, especially if organizational processes continue to run smoothly. In both the literal and figurative cases, the action of *greasing the wheels* involves an individual's taking steps to ensure smooth functioning. Throughout the book, metaphors are used to capture the characteristics of exemplary facilitators.

GLOB OF GLUE, BUTTERFLY, CHAMELEON, AND IMPLEMENTATION GENIUS

As I described the facilitator role to professional colleagues and interviewed participants and supervisors, I heard several terms, some quite creative, used within their organization to describe this role. Bob, the director of a medical clinic, described Adam as a *glob of glue*. The nickname was earned due to his friendly, positive presence and his ability to bring together people of diverse clinic roles, training, and opinions to work toward a common goal.

Ryan shared the term *expediter* from the food industry. In restaurants, this person interfaces between the wait staff and kitchen staff to help things flow smoothly. The expediter helps organize food orders, communicates between the two groups, and can decrease stress during busy phases by anticipating needs of waiters and chefs and providing a lighthearted, stabilizing presence.

Lionel, a healthcare system executive and supervisor, claimed the *butterfly* role was essential for organizational success. Not anchored to one department of a system, this person is able to float among independent silos (isolated subdivisions) of an organization and understand how the parts are interconnected, much like a butterfly floats from one flower to the next. In a similar vein, Katie used the term *airplane* to describe her role in a medical clinic. She and her supervisor created the airplane metaphor to describe her role of "flying" over the work groups in disparate parts of the clinic. From that higher perspective she sees the gestalt—how the parts are connected. Her understanding of the system enables her to be more effective with process improvement efforts.

Jean's supervisor, Kris, described her as an *implementation genius*.[5] According to Kris, "We consider Jean to be an 'implementation genius.' She has this remarkable ability to take complex and divergent landscapes where there are very strong opinions, and has the ability to put that into a framework or a process that ultimately gets to resolution."

Claire, a longtime employee in a car dealership, stated, "I'm kind of a *chameleon*, able to adapt and understand what the customer is needing... and from coworkers. If they're shorthanded, I have no problem picking up a soap brush and cleaning a car; I am also able to communicate processes, like in our sales department, I've been able to jump into roles...being a little more adaptable."

"I'm known as a *doer*," reported Lynn. "If they need something done and done quickly, they typically task that to me because that's just the way I work, my personality....I don't like it to linger....I like to get it done."

Alice described herself as a *worker bee*, being efficient and focusing on tasks.

Rich described his role in one word: "I am an *ambassador*. In this role you've got to be a people person; you've got to have a servant's heart...not everybody who walks in the door is happy....you have to be able to put yourself in their shoes. I meet the customer....I greet them. I get basic information for the service advisors. And then I do a lot of other things. If other employees may be struggling, they may need some encouragement; I print out daily schedules, make copies, and give them to the porters...so I'm kind of this all-purpose person. But the most important part is that the customer is greeted in a prompt, friendly way."

Katie's supervisor reflected that her coworkers, particularly those with less training and less self-confidence, may see Katie as a *lifeguard*. "I think they would see her as a lifeguard. She's the one who is really looking out for them and is an advocate for them....when there are stresses going on in the clinic, she is the one who helps defuse it."

Sandy's supervisor described her as an emotional *sponge*. "She is very kind and quite bold in her caring in a very positive way....she will in good humor talk about the stress of the group. But it's sort of a good sponge for the stress."

The exemplary facilitators' job titles (see Table 2, p. 26), some described metaphorically, varied among the organizations. But their actions made processes easier for others. During the interviews, common themes started to emerge, such as a systems awareness, compassion, empathy, finding common ground, and a desire to take action.

MORE THAN PROJECT MANAGEMENT TECHNIQUES

Project managers have the formal training to move projects and processes forward. They typically have a wide range of tools to help teams accomplish goals. Despite training and tools, however, some project managers lack the full range of skills needed to make the change process *easier* for others. Let's consider the cases of Carrie and Dawn so you can see what I mean.

Carrie, a consulting project manager from the information systems division, was assigned to our hospital department. Our collective goal was to update the outdated personnel evaluation system, moving from paper forms to a more efficient online format. Carrie provided sophisticated project management tools to document and track our progress. But early in the process, relationships became strained. Carrie hadn't taken the time to build rapport and get to know us; she jumped in and tried to drive the process changes. But that left our team feeling as if we were working for the consultant rather than collaborating. Power struggles ensued. Meetings were stressful; team members avoided them when possible. The project dragged out for many months. The results were mediocre.

Dawn, on the other hand, was an external project management consultant hired with grant funds. The project goal was to implement process improvement strategies in a primary care medical clinic. Her initial sessions with the leaders and managers were aimed at identifying their highest priorities for change. The leaders brainstormed and came up with several potential projects: reducing physician paperwork, improving the efficiency of referrals to specialists, and communicating laboratory test results to patients in a shorter time. Initially, the group was very excited about the potential changes. The enthusiasm waned, however, as Dawn urged the group to change priorities to those aligned with other regional clinics. It became more apparent that she had a different agenda than the clinic leaders. She had difficulty communicating her position with transparency. Group trust eroded, and process change slowed to a standstill. Eventually a different consultant was assigned, delaying the process by several months.

Being involved in both of these cases, I saw that the project managers, despite adequate technical training, failed as facilitators. Successful facilitation requires a broader set of skills.

The role of facilitators has received considerable research attention in nursing and primary care medical practices. Many investigators have focused on the role and attributes of external practice facilitators. These are experts who come into an organization from the outside on a temporary basis in order to facilitate change, improve processes, and enhance teamwork. Researchers and experts[6] have identified key skills of external facilitators, such as knowledge of how to manage groups and awareness of the change process. In the field of nursing, facilitators are described as people who make things easier for others, promote action, encourage others, and help others achieve specific goals. One group of researchers presented a continuum that captures both the technical skills and the personal attributes of effective facilitators. In their model, the technical or "task" end of the continuum is characterized by practical, task-driven activities such as using tools to support quality improvement projects. In contrast, the "holistic" or relational end of the continuum focuses on relationships and communication skills, such as developing and empowering teams and improving existing organizational culture. The findings of my research apply to both ends of the continuum, although more emphasis is on the relational, holistic soft skills of effective facilitators.

The project management consultants in the two cases presented above offered technical tools. However, their difficulty entering the organizational culture and developing trusting relationships interfered with successful change. While existing research helps in our understanding of external facilitators and how they might improve their effectiveness, less is known about the people within organizations who, in the process of doing their jobs, make things easier for others.

The facilitators described in this book are not external consultants. None were trained to be facilitators. The majority were not project managers. They were selected from different disciplines and filled a variety of roles in diverse organizations. Furthering our understanding of natural facilitators in different functional roles can inform the development of project managers and others involved in change management. "Making things easier for others" can be partially accomplished by introducing technical tools to facilitate change. But the insights gleaned from natural facilitators and their supervisors reveal the personal attributes that make these people successful.

THE VALUE OF UNDERSTANDING FACILITATION

The role of facilitators can go unnoticed or be undervalued. It's not uncommon for a leader or manager to gradually realize that things are "falling through the cracks" or realize only in retrospect, after a key employee is transferred or has left the organization, that teamwork has become problematic. As described in later chapters, facilitators are often humble people who don't want to draw attention to themselves.

Naming and describing this role can help leaders be more intentional in the hiring, retention, and strategic placement of this subtle human asset. During my interview with Dennis, he commented that his job as a college dean has become significantly easier, and he can focus his energy on important leadership issues, since hiring Linda two years ago. His previous executive assistant was competent and performed her duties adequately. However, the facilitation and interpersonal skills Linda brought to the job, beyond the standard job duties, clearly made a difference. But some of those subtle skills were difficult for Dennis to define in succinct, concrete terms. Using results from my research and our conversations, he later integrated into the executive assistant job description some of the characteristics of exemplary facilitators, improving his ability to hire people similar to Linda in the future. Dennis also expressed a strong desire to retain Linda as his executive assistant. Other campus leaders were noticing her exemplary skills. She had opportunities to move to other departments, but with newfound awareness of the characteristics of an exemplary facilitator, Dennis was able to comment on her specific traits when providing positive feedback in daily interactions and in formal evaluations, thereby sustaining Linda's job satisfaction and decreasing the chance that she would leave her position.

In addition to hiring and retaining valued employees, leaders possessed of a deeper understanding of exemplary facilitators can place these gifted employees in strategically advantageous positions in the organization. Facilitators gain intrinsic satisfaction from helping others attain goals. They are often willing to help the organization by flexing their job duties. While being conscious not to overload these employees, leaders can look for opportunities to place natural facilitators on curriculum committees, process improvement taskforces, event-planning teams, and other task-oriented groups to increase the chance for success and maximize their contributions to the organization.

Finally, another benefit of defining and understanding the role of facilitators comes from the perspective of facilitators themselves. I have presented this topic at professional conferences on several occasions. After each talk, a few attendees have approached me. They open the discussion stating their appreciation for the information. They note that the personal attributes of facilitators seem to match their own strengths, and they feel validated and affirmed by the content I've covered. They better understand how they contribute to others. However, for a variety of reasons, they are hesitant to move into or remain in formal leadership positions. They express new confidence that they may derive more satisfaction by intentionally seeking supportive roles that match their natural strengths. And they tell me they can be more intentional when looking for jobs that will be satisfying and productive.

As a psychologist, I sometimes comment to clients that it is difficult to make progress on a personal issue if it remains vague and undefined. By naming the issue and understanding its effects, the individual gains a sense of control, makes choices, and sees progress. Similarly, organizational leaders may have a general positive impression about some special employees, but it may be difficult to define or quantify the behavior. By naming the facilitator role and understanding the defining characteristics, both the leader and employee can be more intentional, making choices that benefit the organization and increase the satisfaction of the facilitator. This is employee engagement at its best.

CHAPTER 2

Studying Facilitators
Methods and Participants

My research goal to identify the personal attributes of natural facilitators brought with it several important questions: Does this group of people share similar abilities? Do their strengths differ from leaders and managers? Can they be found in a variety of organizations? To answer these questions, I decided to step through the doors of a variety of successful organizations to interview these unique individuals and the people who supervise them.

> "When you talk, you are only repeating what you already know. But if you listen, you may learn something new."
>
> DALAI LAMA

THE ORGANIZATIONS

As I considered successful organizations to include in the study, I defined success as a mix of longevity (a long history as an organization) and performance excellence based on objective criteria, such as performance awards. Eventually, I selected eleven organizations from a range of sectors. All of the organizations listed in Table 1 met my criteria of longevity and performance excellence. More details about these topnotch organizations are provided in the Appendix.

TABLE 1: Organizations Participating in the Study

Sector	Description	Employees	Facilitators Interviewed
Education	Public university department	560	2
Government	City government	1,600	1
	County government, public works department	189	1
Healthcare	Urban medical clinic #1	89	2
	Urban medical clinic #2	70	2
	Urban medical clinic #3	65	2
	Urban medical clinic #4	60	1
	Rural medical clinic	40	1
Private Business	Car dealership	160	2
	Multinational food corporation, research & development dept.	50	1
Public Utility	Publicly owned electric company	350	2

THE PEOPLE

As my first step, I spoke with a leader within each organization. I asked the leader to identify one or two exemplary facilitators. The following description was provided to help in their selection:

"Identify a person in your organization who is not in a formal leadership position but is effective getting things done, particularly on teams or activities that involve more than one person. When this person is involved, things just seem to flow more easily, with good outcomes. This can be someone who works with customers, administration or admin support, business, tech support, any aspect of the organization, but he/she stands out to you as someone others like to work with and is someone who makes things flow more smoothly while they get things done."

After facilitators were identified by name, I contacted them by email or phone. I invited each one to participate in an interview so I could better understand their role. The following information was provided in the invitation:

"I am conducting a study of people in organizations identified as skilled facilitators. That is, people who are effective at getting things done, such as group projects, working with customers, or process improvement activities. When I spoke with _____ (name of leader), she/he identified you as a skilled facilitator. If you are willing, I would like to schedule a time to conduct a thirty-minute interview with you at your work location. I would also like to record the interview and possibly use clips of the interview at future presentations or publications. The interview questions will be provided to you in advance along with a consent form."

From the eleven organizations, I contacted a total of seventeen employees (the facilitators) who had been hand-selected by leaders. All seventeen agreed to be interviewed. Table 2 provides information about the facilitators. I also interviewed their supervisors. In four cases, one person supervised two of the facilitators; therefore, there were thirteen supervisors for the seventeen selected employees. One supervisor changed jobs during the project and was no longer available to be interviewed, so I ended up interviewing twelve supervisors.

I interviewed the supervisors separately to obtain a second perspective for each facilitator. Speaking with the supervisors was really helpful. Their input validated the interview data collected from the facilitators. Because supervisors interact with a variety of employees, they can identify comparative strengths and weaknesses among employees. Their input added objectivity to the interview data. For example, during interviews, some facilitators appeared self-effacing, downplaying their contributions to teams and their strengths. Their supervisors, on the other hand, appeared very comfortable and objective when describing the facilitators' strengths and contributions.

THE INTERVIEWS

I conducted most interviews face-to-face in a private room at the worksites of the facilitators and their supervisors. Four of the interviews were conducted by phone because the facilitator and their supervisor were located in other states. I provided the interview questions (Table 3) to participants in advance. The interviews ranged from seventeen to thirty-five minutes in length.

TABLE 2: Natural Facilitators Interviewed in the Study

Organization	Position	Gender	Name*
Car dealership	Sales Consultant and Executive Administrative Assistant	F	Claire
Car dealership	Customer Ambassador	M	Rich
City government office	Policy and Project Manager	F	Jean
County government department	Assistant County Engineer	M	Randy
Medical clinic (urban)	Practice Coach	F	Katie
Medical clinic (urban)	Nurse Case Manager	F	Sandy
Medical clinic (urban)	Social Worker	F	Lynn
Medical clinic (urban)	Registration Coordinator	F	Mary
Medical clinic (urban)	Faculty Physician	M	Adam
Medical clinic (urban)	Faculty Physician	F	Ellen
Medical clinic (urban)	Medical Assistant	F	Chris
Medical clinic (rural)	Education Coordinator	F	Carla
Multinational food corp.	Project Manager/Facilitator	F	Alice
University department	Executive Assistant	F	Linda
University department	Associate Dean	F	Susan
Utility company	Facilities Manager	M	Steve
Utility company	Human Resources Director	F	Loren

*Names have been changed to maintain confidentiality of participants.

TABLE 3: Interview Questions

Interview Questions for Facilitators

1. Tell me about your role. What are your activities in a typical day?

2. In order to be effective in your role, what specific things do you need to do well?

3. If someone else were hired to do this job well, what characteristics should they have?

4. When you start work, are there any things you typically do to prepare? Or do you just dive right in?

5. What do you contribute to a team?

6. What brings you satisfaction at work?

7. During meetings, are there certain things you typically notice? That you pick up on?

8. When those around you are stressed, is there anything specific you do to help the situation?

9. Do you aspire to be promoted to a leadership position? Why or why not?

10. Is there a role model in your family that has inspired you in your work? If so, who? And what is it about him/her that you admire?

Interview Questions for Supervisors

1. What role does she/he fill? What are their activities in a typical day?

2. Why did you select this person? Why did they come to mind?

3. In what ways is she/he an exemplary facilitator? What specific qualities do they demonstrate?

4. Any other characteristics that are unique to this individual?

5. What does she/he contribute to a team?

6. If I were to ask peers about this person, what would they say?

7. How does she/he respond to stressful work situations? How does she/he interact with others during such times?

8. What brings her/him satisfaction at work?

During interviews, I encouraged the participants to be specific with their descriptions. Supervisors, in particular, often responded initially with broad phrases such as, "She communicates well" or, "He is good at collaboration." In those instances, I probed for more specific terms with follow-up questions such as, "What does that look like?" or, "Can you say more about that?" The subsequent descriptions typically were more detailed. They often included behavioral examples, such as, "In a group, she makes positive comments about the input of other group members." The detailed descriptions resulted in more accurate data analysis and, ultimately, a clearer picture of the personal attributes of facilitators.

THE DATA

I transcribed the recorded interviews into typewritten pages then analyzed each transcript to identify characteristics that were mentioned either by the facilitator or their supervisor. I specifically looked for patterns or themes within the data—characteristics that were mentioned frequently. While reviewing the transcripts, I created an initial coding framework and continued to modify it as I read and re-read the transcripts. Initial codes were assigned to all characteristics discussed by the facilitators and their supervisors. For example, the characteristic of being "detail-oriented" would be credited to a facilitator if that characteristic was mentioned by either the facilitator describing their own behavior during the interview or the supervisor describing the facilitator in a separate interview. After I completed the initial coding of the transcripts, I was helped by a professional colleague to make sure my coding system made sense. She independently reviewed ten of the recorded interviews using my coding system. When we compared our ratings, we had agreed on eighty-nine percent of the codes, which meets the approved research standard. Those characteristics mentioned by either the facilitator or the supervisor in at least half of the cases (nine, or fifty-three percent, of the sample of seventeen facilitators) are included in the following chapters.

The final step of my research was to create accurate descriptive labels for each characteristic. During my initial coding process described above, I used general terms such as "organized" or "friendly." But I wanted more detailed labels that captured the characteristics more accurately. I went back to the transcripts to find the words used in the interviews. For some characteristics, I inserted my own terms to add more depth to the label. Finally, I sought others' opinions to refine the labels. When I presented the preliminary results at two separate continuing education conferences, I showed samples from the interviews, grouped by theme, and my proposed descriptive label for each characteristic. Members of the audience provided written and verbal comments to improve the labels. Using their feedback, combined with my own descriptive terms, I finalized the labels, which are shown as the first two words of the titles in the following chapters and in the table below.

THE RESULTS

Seven characteristics met the inclusion criterion: they were mentioned during interviews by either the facilitator or their supervisor in at least fifty percent of the cases. Table 4 lists the characteristics. The following chapters describe each characteristic in more detail.

TABLE 4: Characteristics of Natural Facilitators

Characteristic	Frequency (of 17 facilitators)
Completing tasks	14 (82%)
Being organized	14 (82%)
Being perceptive	17 (100%
Having a positive presence	17 (100%)
Remaining calm	17 (100%)
Genuinely caring	17 (100%)
Offering a systems awareness	10 (59%)

CONFIDENTIALITY

To maintain confidentiality, I changed the names of the natural facilitators and their supervisors. For those interested, I can provide further information about the consent form and the approval by an institutional review board. Other than changing participant names, all other information, including direct quotes, has not been altered.

WHAT'S NEXT:

Part Two describes the personal attributes of natural facilitators. Also referred to as characteristics or strengths, these attributes were mentioned by the facilitators or their supervisors in the majority of interviews. When you "look under the hood" of exemplary facilitators, here is what you will find.

IMPORTANT POINTS FROM PART ONE

In Part One I introduce the concept of natural facilitators, explain why they are valuable to organizations, and describe how our understanding of these valuable employees was increased by interviewing facilitators and their supervisors in successful organizations. Here's a summary of important points from the first part:

- Natural facilitators have not been trained in facilitation methods, yet they make processes easier for others or the organization; in the process of doing their assigned jobs, they help to make things go "smoother" or "more easily" for others; they enable others to do their jobs better; they support the decision-makers.

- Facilitators can be overlooked. Sometimes their value is not recognized until after they leave a position and things don't go as smoothly.

- Examples of natural facilitators can be found wherever people interact, including diverse work environments, families, and sports.

- A primary purpose of this book is to help leaders and managers recognize the value and characteristics of natural facilitators. This information can be used when hiring and retaining these valued employees and by placing them in strategically advantageous positions in the organization.

- Natural facilitators can use this information to build a sense of identity and pride, and to recognize how they contribute to others and the organization. They can be more intentional about choosing jobs that will be satisfying and productive.

- Facilitation means "to make things easier."

- Metaphors such as a butterfly, chameleon, expediter, and glob of glue are often used to identify facilitators in work environments.

- The personal attributes of natural facilitators go beyond project management techniques; their relational, holistic soft skills empower teams and improve organizational culture.

- Natural facilitators bring value in several ways: they help projects get completed, they help groups work together, they help leaders and the organization be more successful.

- Information for this book came, in part, by interviewing seventeen natural facilitators and their supervisors selected from eleven successful organizations.

- To find natural facilitators in the selected organizations, leaders were asked to identify individuals who are the best (exemplary) at getting things done and working with others.

PART TWO

Attributes of
Natural Facilitators

CHAPTER 3

Completing Tasks
Getting It Done, One Bite at a Time

Natural facilitators derive satisfaction from completing tasks and projects. They are adept at working with other individuals and groups to move toward a common goal. Many take pride in their ability to multitask. They apply a variety of methods to get projects started, maintain momentum, and track progress. Some are talented at helping groups analyze options and solve problems. When organizational goals are identified, a facilitator often kicks into gear, either voluntarily or by assignment, to move the process forward. This is a core characteristic of facilitators. They instinctively attend to process—how to get things done.

"An idea not coupled with action will never get any bigger than the brain cell it occupied."

ARNOLD GLASOW,
AMERICAN BUSINESSMAN

Task-oriented or *action-oriented* are appropriate descriptors for this attribute. Rather than create goals or manage personnel, facilitators prefer to take action on specified problems or targets. Because they often break down large goals into manageable steps, the question posed in the humorous metaphor, "How do you eat an elephant?" is answered by the actions of facilitators, "One bite at a time."

A primary component of taking action is getting new projects off the ground. Several natural facilitators stated they are the ones who "dive in" and *initiate action* when a new project is identified. Getting projects started is a crucial step in any change process. Many times over my career I've witnessed a work group or executive committee agree on a new, creative idea—only to have it stall because nobody follows through. Even if someone is identified to start the change process, they may not have the skill or interest to take the very first concrete steps to move the process forward. Initiating action is where many natural facilitators excel. They don't like projects to linger. They like to get a project moving and willingly step in to get it kickstarted. Read the comments on pages 38 and 39 to find how the facilitators and their supervisors describe this tendency.

Another component of taking action is *maintaining momentum*. When the initial energy dwindles, projects can stagnate. Like many New Year's resolutions, the initial appeal wears thin, and the plan falls to the wayside. The odds of success are improved when someone persists and keeps track of a project. Natural facilitators keep projects moving. Persistence can take the form of verbal or written reminders. I recall a humorous comment by a colleague years ago, addressed to an exemplary facilitator in our department, "You are like a dog holding on my pant leg—you won't let go!" As that comment reflects, it may require some tenacity to keep a project moving. Along with persistence, facilitators described a variety of methods they use to keep projects on track. Again, they are not trained to keep the ball rolling. They're just naturally good at it.

In addition to initiating action and maintaining momentum, exemplary facilitators help to complete tasks by *finding solutions* along the way. They do this in a couple of ways. One is by managing group discussions and probing for ideas from others. They have the unique ability to harness group energy and, without blame, dissect problems and consider options. This strength helps avoid a common pitfall of new initiatives and projects—one or two people end up shouldering the responsibility for everyone else. When this happens, it becomes an individual project rather than a team project; the input of the team is lost. The ability of facilitators to solicit ideas from others ensures that problems are "owned" and solved by the team. During interviews, facilitators recognized their ability to remain objective and help the team stay focused on the end goal without getting sidetracked.

Another way that facilitators help to find solutions is by assisting leaders to think through problems. Bruce, a residency program director, relied on Ellen to help him analyze complex problems. In confidential discussions, he valued her ability to ask insightful questions and share her objective observations. In this manner, Ellen, a facilitator, helped Bruce, the leader, by collaborating to solve problems. Supervisors used terms such as "objective" and "analytical" thinker to describe facilitators.

Participating in a successful project is highly satisfying to facilitators. It is gratifying for them to witness a group working together toward a common goal. As planning moves forward, they enjoy checking off items that have been accomplished. They take part in the action. They are willing to do their share of the work. They will step in to record minutes at a committee meeting; they will follow up with their assigned tasks. It is apparent that facilitators gain satisfaction from their role and from seeing tangible results from their efforts. On pages 46 and 47 are some responses to the question: What brings you satisfaction at work?

To recap the characteristic of being task-oriented, exemplary facilitators have a natural interest in taking action on defined projects or processes. They initiate action, often being the first ones out of the gate, focusing on practical steps to get a project started. They maintain momentum through persistence, issuing reminders, and tracking progress for the group. Finally, they excel at helping others find solutions along the way by soliciting group input as well as collaborating with leaders by sharing their objective, analytical insights.

BENEFITS OF A TASK ORIENTATION

Positioning facilitators to participate in task-oriented activities offers several benefits. At the top of the list is job satisfaction for these valuable employees. They enjoy this type of work. Supporting successful projects is intrinsically satisfying to them. It increases the likelihood they will stay in

About initiating action

"When we come up with the ideas, and the things to be done, I typically am the person who jumps in, who starts it off."

— MARY

"The ability to take a task and get it done. That's how I'm known. I think here at the clinic if they need something done and done quickly, they typically task that to me because that's just the way I work, my personality. I'm a doer. If I were to get a task, I don't like it to linger, I don't like to wait for days, I like to get it done. Being a doer, I'm very task-oriented, so I want to know how are we going to get from where we are now to moving forward."

— LYNN

"I get very frustrated with someone who is leading a meeting or leading a project doesn't have that (an action plan). I say 'Let's just get to it. What do we need to do to get this done?'"

— ALICE

"One thing that bugs me in a meeting is, if we're talking about a certain topic, I want there to be an action plan—what are we going to actually do? So sometimes I'll throw that out: 'OK, now what's the action plan? We gotta do something now.'"

— SANDY

"I'll just jump in and help, I guess. I want to know how I can fix it. 'What are we going to do to fix it?'"

— CLAIRE

"I'm one of the people that before the meeting disbands will say, 'Wait a minute, who is going to be the person responsible for x, y, and z? Who's going to make sure that that happens?' I'm always surprised how often that falls by the wayside and is not done."

— ELLEN

NATURAL FACILITATORS

About facilitators initiating action

"She is able to listen to a long, arduous conversation by a bunch of physicians working on a project and really distill out the key pieces of the things that need to be done and move a project along. It means that she's the first one out of a meeting to be able to figure out what has to get done to promote the project."

— SANDY'S SUPERVISOR

"She's definitely more of a task person, no question. Claire is more of a 'Let's look at follow-up and come up with a good system. OK, we'll work together and we'll find a system.' She's good at process."

— CLAIRE'S SUPERVISOR

"So she's asking good questions in a 'make things better, continuous improvement' mode, more so than 'Let's think about where we should be five years from now.'"

— JEAN'S SUPERVISOR

"They both have the great ability to dive in and get work done."

— LYNN AND MARY'S SUPERVISOR

About maintaining momentum

"It really is a lot of the time you're playing the middle man, you're helping facilitate getting things done, but it's somebody else's project that you're helping them to build. So there are a lot of things that have to get organized, tracking when projects get completed. I enjoy that part, of keeping things on track."

— RANDY

"Keeping all the tasks associated with any project straight is important. Implementing project management tools is important. One that I use a lot is a project matrix. It lists all the projects we're working on, all the due dates, deliverables, who's working on what."

— KATIE

"I have a timeline for all that I need to accomplish, and that helps me keep on track and to help the people I'm working with keep on track and that we're progressing towards a goal and getting things done in the time we have."

— ELLEN

"And also push a little bit. Assign somebody. Pestering them in a nice way to get things done. Yeah, to kind of move things ahead. Trying to get things assigned for action items. Yeah, sometimes I'm often the person taking minutes and sending them around."

— SUSAN

"I wouldn't have the answer but help to bring the group back to what the question was, to keeping the group on task—getting meetings set up and the right people are invited to the meetings, and reminders that there is a meeting, and, at the meeting, trying to help keep them on task."

— CARLA

"It's easy for me to think, 'What is the end goal and how do we get there?' That comes easy for me. I facilitate a lot of projects and keep projects on track."

— LINDA

"To make sure that everyone is accountable, working with some intention to get things done. Momentum comes to mind. They are the ones that keep the momentum going in different realms."

— KATIE AND SANDY'S SUPERVISOR

"So, getting work done themselves, supporting others to do the work, and following up to keep the team moving. Absolutely, they will follow up. Whenever there are team meetings or group projects, they will follow up via email, they will wander around and check in with team members, they will communicate their progress on tasks that have been assigned to them."

— LYNN AND MARY'S SUPERVISOR

their job. Their satisfaction is contagious and improves the morale of those around them.

As noted earlier, facilitators maintain momentum and monitor the progress of projects. Tracking and documenting progress, even small successes, can have a positive effect on group morale. This is especially true if leaders and managers recognize the opportunity to closely track the progress and communicate the positive results to the larger organization. Positive outcomes, regardless of magnitude, provide opportunities for recognition and celebration.

Finally, another obvious benefit of the task orientation of exemplary facilitators is improved outcomes, such as streamlined processes, successful events, and accomplished goals.

At the midpoint of my career, I was on the faculty of a family medicine residency program. Our program held strategic planning retreats. During these annual events, twelve faculty members typically brainstormed several lofty, complex goals for the coming year. Despite the best of intentions, limited progress was made in the months following the retreat. Everyone was extremely busy. Other daily duties took priority. With heroic effort and extra hours, some goals were accomplished by individual faculty members. But the risk of burnout was real. Many elements of the strategic plan were only partially accomplished.

Then one year the director restructured the faculty job duties. Kevin's job duties were modified to include protected time for project development. Several months later, at the next strategic planning retreat, the faculty once again identified a compelling goal: a major revision of the training curriculum around the concept of a *master clinician*. That is, the faculty envisioned the broad competencies to be demonstrated by a resident physician upon completion of training; they created a clear picture of the end product. In the words of Jim Collins,[7] the faculty identified a "big, hairy, audacious goal." To attain this goal, each faculty member would need to review and revise an assigned portion of the curriculum. It would be an intense, time-consuming process. After identifying the broad goals for the revised curriculum, the faculty concluded the retreat with renewed excitement and enthusiasm.

In the following weeks and months, Kevin, as the project developer, established a step-by-step process. He scheduled individual and small-group meetings. Working with individual faculty members, he established realistic timelines. He reminded people about upcoming deadlines and created a flowchart to document progress. Momentum was maintained. Progress reports became a standard agenda item at weekly faculty meetings. Innovative evaluation methods were implemented. The eventual outcome was a competency-based curriculum, built around the "master clinician" concept envisioned by the faculty two years earlier. Viewed as a success, the curriculum model was presented by faculty members at two national conferences and published in a professional journal.

Creating a project developer role made all the difference. Kevin, with no formal project management training, was a natural facilitator. Broad goals were broken down into manageable steps. In this support role, the facilitator initiated action by scheduling meetings, keeping records, reminding others of the project, and maintaining momentum. The facilitator's personal attribute of being task-oriented was vital for the success of the two-year project, one bite at a time.

About finding solutions

"I've been able to just listen and then go, 'OK, let's talk about this. What is the best way, what are we looking to accomplish to fix the problem?' Instead of escalating it. Kind of like being an advisor for the situation. Maybe we messed up. Just getting down to the root of the problem and then solving that."

— CLAIRE

"I like solving problems—not personnel problems, necessarily, but project problems. I think as much as anything it's that sense of accomplishment, to be able to complete a task."

— RANDY

"Yeah, as far as logistical thinking and problem solving, I think I'm very good at that."

— LINDA

"But I think my strength is in the options stage. Let's talk about how we're going to get there, let's really bounce around ideas for options to figure out how to do it."

— JEAN

"What about that situation is causing the stress? Kind of a root-cause analysis to get to what the issue is."

— CARLA

"I think I bring objectivity to the team. Again, I am enough removed that I really see my role as a problem solver."

— KATIE

About facilitors finding solutions

"She just has this remarkable ability to take complex and divergent landscapes where there's very strong opinions, and she has the ability to put that into a framework or a process that ultimately gets to resolution. In her heart she is a problem solver. She's a problem solver in these wickedly complex situations and finding a path forward. Her teams make measurable progress."

— JEAN'S SUPERVISOR

"And then she really thinks well on her feet in terms of facilitating ideas during sessions.... She can take a step back and take...various ideas that participants have contributed, and figure out how to cluster them....what are the key ideas."

— ALICE'S SUPERVISOR

"She is very analytical and very quick to be able to dissect problems and come up with ideas about how to move forward....Which is very valuable for me to listen to when problems come up because that's a skill that is pretty unique. Not everybody has that."

— ELLEN'S SUPERVISOR

"She's also a great problem solver. When we can't get alignment for something to occur, she time and again figures out ways to tackle an issue and solve it, and not upset people."

— LINDA'S SUPERVISOR

"What brings you satisfaction at work?"

"And I like supporting the people who are doing that work. That's very fulfilling for me. I like to see if they have wins and successes in the clinic. If they've had stumbling blocks or barriers, and being able to overcome those and progress in whatever it is they're working on is really satisfying for me."

— KATIE

"For me I get a lot of satisfaction leading a team through a process and helping them complete that process, whether I'm facilitating it or part of the team, from start to finish."

— ALICE

"I enjoy helping develop processes or being part of a team that develops processes to help people work more effectively and efficiently. Whenever that happens, it's a high satisfier."

— CARLA

"I really enjoy seeing projects through; being part of a successful project or successful event."

— LINDA

"I like to accomplish things. Again, I get more satisfaction seeing the work get accomplished."

— RANDY

"I think checking things off, like when a new faculty member has a successful proposal and I feel like I helped."

— SUSAN

"What brings him/her satisfaction at work?"

"Seeing work processes improve or an outcome improve is really rewarding, and they are happy to put significant time and energy into things like that."
— LYNN AND MARY'S SUPERVISOR

"I think it's seeing projects that are completed; knowing that she managed a project that came out with a successful outcome."
— LINDA'S SUPERVISOR

"And I think she gets a lot of satisfaction from just getting things done."
— ALICE'S SUPERVISOR

"Accomplishing things. Doing work on projects and doing something tangible and long-lasting."
— RANDY'S SUPERVISOR

CHAPTER 4

Being Organized
Checklists and Schedules and Notes, oh My!

The terms *organized* and *detailed* came up in the great majority of interviews. Most facilitators keep "to do" lists and derive satisfaction from crossing items off the list. Some chuckled self-consciously, self-disclosing that perhaps they were too well-organized. But most explained that their system helps them keep track of their various responsibilities.

> "Ellen is very detail-oriented, a very organized individual....That's one of her unique skills; she's very excellent in that regard."
>
> ELLEN'S SUPERVISOR

The phrase "They can't see the forest for the trees" is often used to describe people who get caught up in details and don't see the bigger picture. Some of the facilitators took this metaphor to a new level. Not only do they focus on the trees, but they arrange the trees in straight rows, lined up according to their size and species. For example, many facilitators keep two lists: one for daily tasks and a second for long-term projects. Some keep three or more lists. This strong tendency to focus on details benefits the organization. The big-picture thinkers and visionaries, as well as everyday workers, can be successful because the trees receive attention. Important items don't fall through the cracks because a facilitator attends to the details of projects and processes.

Another benefit of being organized is the ability to anticipate needs. Because most facilitators keep schedules for projects, they are constantly looking ahead and preparing for the next steps. Again, this helps processes flow more smoothly. Meetings are scheduled in a timely manner, the right people are invited to attend, minutes are completed, agendas are prepared in advance, purchases are made, the right equipment is available, funds are deposited, grant reports are submitted—the list is endless.

Chris is a medical assistant. She is responsible for walking a patient from the waiting room to an examination room, obtaining preliminary information such as the patient's stated concerns and vital signs, and, following the office visit, preparing the room for the next patient. The clinic director identified Chris as an employee who "gets things done." Due to Chris's busy schedule, we arranged our meeting a month in advance.

On the morning of our interview, Chris greeted me as we settled into a small meeting room in the medical clinic. I noted that she had thoughtfully prepared a glass of water for each of us. In her mid-twenties, she appeared a little nervous but was friendly and alert. When I asked about the typical start of her day, she explained, "I arrive about a half hour before clinic starts, as early as I can, to make sure I get all my tasks done before clinic, so I have time to organize and prioritize my tasks for the day. I make a little checklist, look at my daily schedule." I probed for more details. "I have a routine that I follow every day pretty much when I walk into clinic. I turn certain lights on, make sure the trash cans are in the right place in each exam room." I asked how that routine started. "Over time, I figured out what people would need before clinic that would make things run more smoothly. I'm also very detail-oriented. I kind of double check people's work just to make sure everything is going well, especially for our new hires."

Chris developed these work habits on her own. No one asked her to come in early, to organize the exam rooms, or to check on the work quality of newly hired employees. She naturally takes on these responsibilities. Her attention to detail is clearly evident in her daily routine.

The tracking methods described by the facilitators, such as making lists and using matrices, were organic. That is, the individual developed them over time to meet their unique needs. None mentioned the use of commercially available or sophisticated electronic organizers. Rather, they used simple handwritten lists or readily available computer programs to maintain lists or organize emails. As I mentioned earlier, some used two lists, one for daily tasks and another for long-term projects. To prioritize this organization and planning, several facilitators described carving out protected time, typically at the beginning of the day, prior to the onset of normal business activities.

As it happens, the organizational habits of the facilitators match those recommended by experts to enhance personal and organizational productivity. In his book *Getting Things Done*, David Allen[8] offers several tips to help people manage commitments and tasks. For example, any task you consider unfinished must be captured in a trusted system that is outside your mind and you can come back to sort through (such as an active "to do" list). Also, you must keep reminders of these unfinished tasks in a system to be reviewed regularly, both on a daily basis for current tasks and a weekly basis for current projects. Allen's organizing strategies seemed to come naturally to the facilitators. Unaware of his book, they simply integrated his recommended practices into their daily work habits.

In fact, some supervisors spontaneously commented that this trait appears to be innate for these individuals. Again, their tendency to organize and attend to detail seems to come naturally.

Quotes from the facilitators and their supervisors show the near-universality of this characteristic of being *organized* and *detail-oriented*.

Of course, getting organized takes time. Several facilitators commented on their habit of arriving early to work. Similar to Chris's early-morning routine in the medical clinic, the extra time allows them to be organized and fully prepared for the day and their responsibilities.

About being organized

"I am a very organized person. And that has also been a very important skill for me. And so I keep lists of what needs to be done and make sure that I have a timeline for all that I need to accomplish."

— ELLEN

"Definitely being organized, and being able to keep track of paperwork; having checklists for every main activity. I am definitely a planner."

— CARLA

"Oh, I'm very organized. I would say about an 8 or 9. I have spreadsheets...I keep lists; my file folders are all labeled, so if staff need forms they come into my office; so I'm very organized."

— CLAIRE

"What do I bring to a team? I think maybe that sense of organization."

— SUSAN

"I have to be extremely organized, very detail-oriented. I have a very organized in-box. Uh, maybe a little too organized (laughs)....I have an actual hard copy 'to do' list that I write down and cross off, and I update it every day."

— LINDA

"Because I have so many projects going on at the same time, I make 'to do' lists. I'm big on checking things off my 'to do' list."

— MARY

"I'm much more on the detail side. I have different lists; I usually have a list of things I know I have to accomplish over the next week or month. And then each day I try to make sure I write down what I've got to get done that day."

— RANDY

"I look at my calendar for the day, and I project it out for two to three days and what's coming up the next week. I'm always checking back on that project tracking matrix, and then I keep lists. I have a project list whiteboard in my office."

— KATIE

"You have to be organized."

— SANDY

"I think I'm the queen multitasker. I make a list of my day, and I know what I have to do during the day, and then I look at the list at the side of projects I can complete as well, if I have time. So I have my 'to do' list and I have my 'other list.' I'm a creature of habit."

— LYNN

About facilitators being organized

"Both Sandy and Katie have an internal organization that is notable.... It's not really something you can teach someone, I think. If we went back to their Girl Scout troops, they were probably known this way as well, you know, from many years ago. It's not something that a course in organization...could teach anyone."

— SUPERVISOR OF KATIE AND SANDY

"Also, she's very organized. Also very proactive."

— SUSAN'S SUPERVISOR

"Claire is really organized....I think it's in her nature to be organized, and the process is always clean....I think that's part of her general nature."

— CLAIRE'S SUPERVISOR

"She had very, very good organizational skills....she had everything so well organized.... In fact, I know that when we had our reviews, they (the external reviewers) would often say when they left our program, 'Wow, that person's good!' She was just a very good organizer."

— CARLA'S SUPERVISOR

"Yeah, he stays on top of things. He tracks a lot of things that are going on."

— RANDY'S SUPERVISOR

"She's also very organized. I had prior to Linda a different individual that did not have the skill set that Linda has. In terms of her organization, I very much value that. She's very much structured, organized."

— LINDA'S SUPERVISOR

About coming in early

"Yes, I'm an opener; I'm an early bird....I like to keep our team happy, so I'll start the morning making sure they have a fresh pot of coffee, hot water for tea, all the brochures are restocked for customers, things like that. That's usually my routine."

— CLAIRE

"I'll just say that the way I start my day, well, I'm just a little anal. I arrive at 7:30 every day; it's about an hour before our patients start to show up, because I feel like I need to get ready for my day."

— LYNN

"I arrive early, as early as I can, to make sure I get all my tasks done before clinic, so I have time to organize and prioritize my tasks for that day. Over time, I figured out what people would need before clinic that would make things run more smoothly."

— CHRIS

"I get here before other people. I like the quiet, and I like kind of getting prepared for my day. I have a very specific way I go through things....So I have a little routine in the manner I do things. I get here early so I get a head start before other people start coming."

— SANDY

"So when I get in...the doors open at 7:30, I get here a little before seven. I print out the listing of the time, the date, the car, the customer name, and the service advisor....So I print out my sheet, then I make copies— six sets. So that's the main thing in the morning, and so I cut them all up, staple them, and then I give them to the porters when they come in.... I have to have this done by about twenty after seven."

— RICH

Three facilitators stated that they are not unusually organized or detail-oriented. They described themselves as average on this characteristic, similar to most employees. Comments from their supervisors, however, suggest the facilitators perhaps have unusually high standards for themselves. Their supervisors viewed them as organized.

"And though he may not say he's organized, he is in many ways; he's very detail-oriented....He is organized, but again, his approach and the way he comes across to others, you might not recognize that."

— ADAM'S SUPERVISOR

"I think she is incredibly organized in terms of the ability to lead group facilitation. She gets the pre-work done, she gets the plan in place....she's just incredibly efficient and effective at follow-up as well."

— ALICE'S SUPERVISOR

"Yes, I would say she is organized and detail-oriented. The reason I'm hesitating is because it's not like some project managers I have seen, where they have a checklist. She's not like that. She hates rigid project management tools. She's organized and detail-oriented to the point of like things are never going to fall through the cracks with her. She's that kind of organized. But she's not like 'give me a twenty-line spreadsheet and...fill it out.'"

— JEAN'S SUPERVISOR

To summarize, being organized and detail-oriented is a strength of exemplary facilitators. They use a range of tools, mostly home-grown by the individual, to keep track of their tasks and projects. They find satisfaction by checking items off the list. In terms of our forests and trees metaphor, facilitators develop systems to ensure that newly planted saplings are watered daily, pruned weekly, and develop into the mature trees needed for the healthy forest that represents the organization. Based on supervisor comments, this attribute is valued and benefits the organization.

CHAPTER 5

Being Perceptive
Absorbing the Social Environment

David is an enthusiastic leader. He is bright, decisive, friendly, informed, and understands the broad issues influencing his discipline. But running a meeting is not his strong suit. When leading a meeting, he routinely slips into the role of a participant rather than facilitator. That is, he speaks at length, provides background information on a topic, and expresses his own opinion, losing awareness of time limitations and the need to elicit input from others. A structured agenda doesn't help. What he lacks is sensitivity to the social environment—the ability to "read the room" and involve others. He has difficulty stepping back from his own inner world, observing the engagement and reactions of group members, asking for input, summarizing the conversation, and keeping the meeting on track. In a word, he has difficulty facilitating. Consequently, the meetings are less productive, often run overtime, and are less satisfying to participants. The cause is not his lack of knowledge or intellectual limitations. Instead, it is related to emotional intelligence—a heightened sensitivity to the social environment.

> "Is she in tune with others? Big time."
>
> SUSAN'S SUPERVISOR

About being perceptive

"I think I have a good sense of emotionally where the people in the room are. And if somebody says something, I do think I pick up faster than others if there's been a misunderstanding or a miscommunication."

— ELLEN

"When I see that there's a person who's not speaking up in a meeting, that always raises my flag a little bit."

— MARY

"I feel like I'm a fairly intuitive person....It's definitely easy to know if they're not paying attention or not engaged."

— LINDA

"I have to be present. have to be able to watch body language and be able to cue into those verbal cues as well; being able to watch folks and be able to tell who's engaged and who isn't."

— LYNN

"I have found one of the best things to have in my reserve is the ability to listen well; I am able to pick up on what people are saying or not saying pretty well, to read the room."

— KATIE

"Reading people; their expressions, eye rolls, posture."

— CLAIRE

"I have a pretty good idea what their personalities are like. I usually can sense that there's something wrong....It's probably that I've worked with people enough to read that."

— RANDY

"And that's one thing that I like to think I do well is I listen. I hear people."

— STEVE

"I notice people's emotions, the vibe they're putting off. I notice if someone is speaking more than normal or not speaking up at all...body language, tone of voice, whether they're jumping right in or withholding."

— CHRIS

"Really, listening and observation skills, because I think you really do need to understand the organization as a whole before you can be super effective."

— JEAN

"I consider myself a pretty good reader of people. Kind of gauging the room, if somebody's not paying attention or somebody is reserved, why are they disengaging from the conversation? How can we bring them back in?"

— LOREN

"I certainly was aware of the body language going on in the room....I think that may be kind of a 'female sense' of clueing into that. I would certainly pick up on if somebody was stressed out."

— CARLA

"I need to understand people well. So I have to...read a room. I have to be able to see and understand people and where they're at."

— ALICE

"And you've got to be able to read people.... I spend a lot of time watching. I can tell when they get out of the car, and they look at me and say the first words, I can tell where they're at."

— RICH

Being *perceptive*, the third characteristic of exemplary facilitators, is the ability to absorb the social environment. Based on interview responses, facilitators are sensitive to what others are thinking and feeling. They pick up on subtle social cues and non-verbal communication, and actively probe for understanding. Several of them have a unique talent for listening to varied input and efficiently organizing the content into themes or categories. The natural tendency to observe, listen, and inquire is a foundational attribute that enables facilitators to work effectively with groups and coworkers.

BEING TUNED IN

Exemplary facilitators are highly attuned to their social surroundings. By observing and listening, they pick up on the feelings and level of engagement of others. The phrase commonly used during interviews was the ability to "read the room." That is, they detect how others are feeling and responding. Other terms that emerged during the interviews included *good listener, intuitive, empathetic*, and *sensitive*.

Being perceptive of others is a cornerstone of emotional intelligence. By sensing others' emotional states or needs, the perceiver is able to adjust or adapt in ways that keep others engaged. For example, verbally acknowledging the input of a cautious, timid committee member ("That's a valuable idea, Steve, thanks for your input") can create a positive sense of being understood and validated and, consequently, increased participation. Probing for more complete understanding from an apparently frustrated team member ("Jane, you seem to have strong feelings about this topic, can you say more?") can lead to new ideas or reveal the need for further discussion, setting the stage for consensus. Respectfully redirecting the conversation away from a long-winded, dominating team member ("Hey John, I can tell you have more to say about this issue, but we need to make sure we hear from everyone. What is your opinion, Cindy?") can keep a discussion flowing without alienating any participants.

Sensitivity to one's social environment is foundational for working successfully with individuals and groups. This characteristic was universally reported by the exemplary facilitators and/or their supervisors.

About facilitators being perceptive

"He's very good at reading people. He can read if someone is in a hurry, he can read if someone is confused, or he can read if they know where they're going. He can read people pretty good, and from there he can help customers how he sees fit."

— RICH'S SUPERVISOR

"And she'll see things sometimes that she'll bring to my attention about a situation being handled in not the best way possible and perhaps not being treated right …but she's just very tuned in to other individuals.…So she's very much tuned in to how others are feeling; she's sensitive to others."

— LINDA'S SUPERVISOR

"(They) listen incredibly well."

— MARY AND LYNN'S SUPERVISOR

"Loren's a great reader of people. I mean, she's got high EQ, very high. Which is good. She will watch and make eye contact, and I enjoy having her in a room even when it's something I'm leading because then I can follow up with her and go, 'I couldn't tell, what do you think? Where are they at?'"

— LOREN'S SUPERVISOR

"She's pretty adaptable and reads the room…I think the energy in the room…reading the room in that 'Are people engaged and is it productive time?'"

— JEAN'S SUPERVISOR

"That's Katie's specialty, so you'll see that as a practice coach, she needs to be someone who is very perceptive of the stress of the clinic."

— KATIE'S SUPERVISOR

EMPATHY

Empathy, based on sensitivity to others, is the ability to see the world from another's viewpoint; to understand another person's experience by trying to place oneself in their position. The phrase commonly used in the interviews was to put oneself "in the shoes" of another. Empathy helps a facilitator anticipate the needs of others. Shifting mentally to another's position sets the stage to meet needs efficiently. Moreover, empathy, along with emotional self-management (described in chapter 7), are two core social competencies required to be effective in the fine art of interpersonal relationships. Studies in work environments consistently show that high performers are able to see things from the perspective of others.[9]

Evidence of empathy can be as simple as the thoughtful planning shown by Chris, the medical assistant described in the previous chapter. Prior to my arrival for the interview at her worksite, she had reserved an office space for our meeting and prepared a fresh glass of water for me. It was a hot summer day. By thinking of my situation, she anticipated my need. It was a simple gesture that I appreciated. Empathy is a form of "being perceptive" that was described by several of the exemplary facilitators and their supervisors.

SEEKING TO UNDERSTAND

Inquiry is another method of absorbing the social environment. It is the active process of getting information from others in order to attain greater understanding. In a group setting, inquiry can add to the collective understanding of all. The most common form of inquiry is asking questions. In addition, facial expression, eye contact, tone of voice, or other utterances ("Uh-huh") can communicate to others an interest or openness to hear more. Although it can take various forms, inquiry is based on a genuine curiosity for more complete understanding.

An inquiry orientation is in contrast to advocacy.[10] To advocate is to present one's viewpoints (thoughts, feelings, opinions, etc.) with the intention of influencing others. Inquiry and advocacy are both aspects of everyday communication. Others have described a similar model of interpersonal communication in organizations but use the terms *pulling* and *pushing*. Inquiry

About empathy

"I think being a mother of three fairly sensitive daughters makes me put myself in other people's shoes more than before I was a mother. So thinking about another person's perspective and how another person is feeling about something makes me be a better employee and a better team member too because I can empathize with others and understand what they're going through."

— MARY

"It's all about the people, and you've got to be able to relate to them. Number one, you've got to be willing to put yourself in their shoes. If you don't do that, you're not going to be able to connect with them and where they are."

— RICH

"I feel like I pick up on other people's stress rather easily; I'm a fairly empathetic person. If I know they are stressed, I'll ask 'Hey, are you OK? What's going on?' and I'll give them a chance to vent."

— CHRIS

"You have to have a lot of empathy. I would say empathy is my strongest quality....It's the interactions that I have with my patients; just seeing...what's meaningful to them. You know, I may have a goal for a patient not to miss their dialysis appointment, but that's not their goal at all, and I have to focus on their goal and help them with that."

— SANDY

"My personal skills and strengths come from looking at situations from the other's perspective of how is this going to impact people?"

— LOREN

"I'm kind of a chameleon, and able to adapt and understand what the customer is needing....I like to treat everyone the same, regardless if it's a big purchase financially. And that whatever (financial) level you're on, I'm going to relate from where you're coming from, and I can put myself in your shoes."

— CLAIRE

"You have to be able to keep in mind that people are really invested in what it is they're working on and very passionate about it; and though I may not always agree, I always honor the fact that that's where they're at. I try to meet a person where they're at."

— KATIE

SUPERVISOR COMMENTS   About the empathy of facilitators

"They're both really considerate and thoughtful of others, too. They both think very clearly about how their actions and words will come across to others, how decisions will impact others. So when they think or speak, others pay attention to them because of that."

— ELLEN AND ADAM'S SUPERVISOR

is pulling, drawing information from others, whereas advocacy is pushing information toward others. In a study I conducted with colleagues, we explored the effects of pushing and pulling in administrative meetings.[11] When disagreements occurred in meetings, the most typical response from leaders was to push, or advocate, for their position. In those cases, the disagreement ended when others accepted or acquiesced to the leader's opinion. On the other hand, a consensus outcome was more likely when the leader pulled, or used inquiry, to get the opinions of others. These results suggest that inquiry is an effective approach to facilitate group process when there are differences of opinion, particularly when a consensus is the desired outcome. With their tendency to inquire, facilitators are well-prepared to help a group come to a consensus.

Statements in the interviews support the observation that natural facilitators are much more likely to inquire than advocate. That is, they observe, listen, and ask to understand, but are less likely to try to push a position to influence others. They are more likely to pull than push. Based on interview responses, the intent of the inquiry is to collect more complete information to present back to the group or other leaders for decision-making. Examples of inquiry were plentiful, as shown on the next page.

Examples of advocacy, on the other hand, were less frequent in the interviews. Several exemplary facilitators described examples of advocating on behalf of others, such as navigating patients through a healthcare system or standing up for fellow employees encountering an HR issue. One facilitator, recently promoted to a mid-manager position, collected employee input and became their "voice" as he pushed their needs to those higher in the organization. As suggested by these examples, facilitators are able to gather input from others, package it, and communicate it on their behalf. However, they are less likely to present their own opinions or ideas with the intention of influencing others. In the interviews, there were no examples of advocacy typically ascribed to leaders, such as creating interest in an idea, initiating change in a process, speaking to groups, or attempting to influence others collectively or individually. Digging deeper, interview data suggested two possible rea-

About the use of inquiry to improve understanding

"*Oftentime in groups, I notice if someone is maybe dominating the conversation and somebody else is wanting to speak up but is not or has checked out. And I'll make it a point to say, 'It looks like you have a thought' or 'It looks like you're wanting to say something, let's put it on the table, let's explore it.' I feel like that's really an essential skill.*"

— KATIE

"I think you need to be able to ask questions. I also make a point to say, 'We've heard from a bunch of people. I want to make sure everyone gets their voice in.'"

— JEAN

"So I focus on who we have at the table and who might need an extra push. An introvert, like myself, they may need a little extra to help us figure this out."

— LYNN

"I think an important skill is just asking questions, to find out more about the situation."

— CARLA

"I try to make sure all the arguments happen. I want to hear all the naysayers; I want to hear all the negative comments people might say about ideas. If I hear grumbling, I try to give opportunities for people to say it, so we can know where everybody stands that we're going to move forward, so we have buy-in from everybody, or at least the chance that they've been heard."

— ADAM

"*Being able to listen. Also just asking questions. Very often I can't really fix it, but I think I can try to be sincere about taking their input and trying to make some progress on something they're concerned about.*"

— SUSAN

"*Making sure that everyone feels comfortable speaking up, getting their input. So if whoever is leading the meeting doesn't notice that, sometimes I'll invite that person into the conversation and ask for their input if they've been quiet.*"

— MARY

About facilitators using inquiry to improve understanding

"*She listens. Another thing she will do is bring out people who are quiet on the team. She'll be listening to people talk about the topic, and if someone is sitting there and hasn't said anything, she will say something like, 'Joe, you haven't said anything recently. Do you have anything you'd like to say?' And then Joe will start talking. And so she made everyone feel heard on the team.*"

— CARLA'S SUPERVISOR

"He solicits input from other people. He wants to hear what they're thinking. He doesn't come in and dominate the conversation. He doesn't say, 'This is what we're going to do.'"

— RANDY'S SUPERVISOR

"Another very high-value skill that Linda has, she is very diligent in trying to understand issues....She's very thorough before she makes any kind of communication."

— LINDA'S SUPERVISOR

sons why facilitators are unlikely to advocate for their own perspective. First, working collaboratively is valued more highly than lobbying for a specific outcome. For some facilitators, it's more important to ensure a collaborative environment in which others create a plan than to have a say in shaping it. They have less interest in deciding the overall direction of a project or getting people on board. Their interest, and talent, is working collaboratively on clearly defined practical problems with boundaries and endpoints. Second, some facilitators experience negative emotional reactions, such as anxiety, when voicing their opinions to groups or participating in potentially tense, advocacy-laden discussions. They are uncomfortable with confrontation. These facilitators may be more willing to contribute their personal viewpoint in a non-contentious environment. Leaders, recognizing that facilitators are reluctant to put forth their personal viewpoint, may need to intentionally invite their input. Likewise, facilitators, especially those moving into leadership positions, may need to further develop their advocacy skills to complement their natural proclivity to inquire. I will say more about developing advocacy skills in chapter 12.

When leading group discussions, some facilitators are skilled at assertively directing the conversation in a productive manner. The goal, in those cases, is to ensure the process is moving forward, not becoming stagnant or sidetracked. Directing a group conversation differs from advocacy when one expresses a viewpoint to influence the content of the conversation.

The vast majority of facilitators described a preference for inquiry to reveal and understand others' viewpoints rather than pushing to influence group opinion. This finding reinforces the picture of exemplary facilitators filling a supportive role. They broaden participation by providing a comfortable, positive forum for others to speak and listen. They enable others to be more successful by smoothing processes, pulling for input, and organizing information so others can generate solutions and make informed decisions.

USING PERCEPTIONS TO ADVANCE GROUP UNDERSTANDING

Several of the exemplary facilitators and their supervisors described advanced group facilitation skills. Building on the ability to "read the room" and inquire for a more complete understanding, they used the resulting information to move a team forward. They are able to summarize a complex conversation and reflect it back to the group. After listening to disparate views of team members, they can identify themes or categories that capture the main points. After respectfully pulling viewpoints from others, they suggest next steps to give the group a unified direction. They summarize, reflect, or reframe perceptions for the benefit of the group. This unusual skill was noticed and valued by supervisors. This skill set, not universal among the people I interviewed, was more typical of those whose job duties included group facilitation.

Interview responses showed that all of the exemplary facilitators are perceptive of their social surroundings. They are sensitive to the experience of others. They are observant; they can "read a room" and frequently inquire for more complete understanding. This characteristic has a positive effect on customers and coworkers. Others feel heard, valued, and validated. Coworkers become more engaged. Group discussions are likely more balanced among participants. New information is considered, shared understanding is possible, and group decisions can be more informed.

About using perceptions to advance group understanding

"Somebody's tone of voice will change a little bit, or their voice will rise a little bit, body language will change, or their facial expression will be a little more guarded. Or they will echo, they'll state back what they think somebody else said, and it will not be what I thought that other person was trying to say. And sometimes being able to rephrase what the original person was saying in a way that the second person, the receiving person, can understand a little better can really be helpful."

— ELLEN

"I recently had somebody tell me, 'You're really good at that. You make people feel heard...you acknowledge what they're saying...and you capture what they're saying, but then you help us move on when we need to move on.'"

— ALICE

"I think I'm fairly open-minded. I can listen to other people's ideas and their thoughts and work things into a nice little package to get to where we need to be based on everybody's input. Just taking everyone's ideas."

— LINDA

About facilitators using perceptions to advance group understanding

"So she has a really remarkable ability...to really be present for people and then also to steer them in a way that becomes constructive instead of destructive. So she's also really good at uncovering the layers beneath something....If we're getting stuck on something, she's able to intervene in redirecting that or calling it to question."

— JEAN'S SUPERVISOR

"Their listening skills, coupled with a great ability to reframe what they've heard, to ask questions and inquire, to communicate clearly, then, whatever those answers are... they're able to inquire and ask questions, or reframe and understand the issue."

— MARY AND LYNN'S SUPERVISOR

" I think Alice has unique talents... facilitating a group in real time. I think she has a sharp sense of intuition... is able to read a group, know what is needed from people to pivot in real time, to drive the group toward interaction and discussion that are going to result in new ideas that wouldn't have been achieved without her sort of leading and orchestrating the group."

— ALICE'S SUPERVISOR

"She was always someone who could sit in the group and listen to everybody talk...and then she would kind of summarize at the end and say, 'What I am hearing people say...' And we would come to a conclusion and a compromise, and then it seemed like the group was happy and everyone left feeling like, 'Hey, we got something accomplished here.' I feel like that's the job of a facilitator, and she made the group feel like they did a good job. I would reiterate that she is good, if she is running a team, at summarizing."

— CARLA'S SUPERVISOR

CHAPTER 6

Having a Positive Presence
Elevating the Team

It's not simply that exemplary facilitators are task-oriented, organized, and tuned in. People enjoy working with them. They are pleasant to be around. They infuse a sense of optimism into a group or team. They acknowledge and appreciate others. They provide a positive presence. Terms pointing to this attribute that emerged during the interviews included *can-do attitude, pleasant, comfortable, friendly, kind, upbeat, energetic, humorous,* and *fun.*

> "So she's good at creating safe spaces and fun and productive environment.... Very genuine, comfortable; it's comfortable to be around her."
>
> JEAN'S SUPERVISOR

This characteristic adds an affective dimension to the description of exemplary facilitators. They not only "get things done" and attend to details; they make the work more enjoyable for others. They interject a positive presence with coworkers and customers. People want them to be on teams. Coworkers like being around them. In addition to the characteristics of action- and detail-oriented, we now include an interpersonal attribute that engenders positive feelings.

In describing this attribute, I intentionally selected the phrase "positive

"What makes you effective?" and "What do you bring to a team?" that connote a positive presence

"I think I bring optimism to our team. I like to keep things light....They would probably say that I am positive; I always have a sense of positivity about myself."

— CHRIS

"Yeah, and having positive professional relationships with my colleagues is important, too. Coming to work and getting along with everyone you work with is really nice. And that goes a long way in any job that you have."

— LINDA

"A lot of it is just being able to like people; to enjoy working with people."

— RANDY

"I appreciate everyone on the team. I try to acknowledge what everyone is bringing....That's just who I am. Yeah, that's something I bring. I always feel bad for the Debbie Downers in the group. Why does it have to be so hard? There are some people, and I have a relationship with them, so it's like, 'It's not really gonna be that bad! We're gonna get this! Stop being a naysayer!' (laughs) But really gently....It's in the moment, a little poking fun, a little irreverence."

— JEAN

"I'm excited about it (medicine), and I really enjoy teaching residents about it. I think that helps me stay engaged in my job, and I think enthusiasm can go a long way for helping get other people engaged."

— ELLEN

"I'm a big cheerleader. I bring positivity, and I always try to start every meeting with kudos…Yeah, just making sure that everybody understands that we're all on the same team, and has that feeling of what it feels like to be on the same team, not just a concept, but a feeling.…I have a pride in the work that everybody does, so I help keep everyone together by pointing out the work that they do."

— ADAM

"I think the number one thing is to make people feel welcome.…Many people who come in are not happy that they're there. Many people are in a hurry; they don't want to wait.…That's the key, to be that welcoming agent, and I literally do that all day long.…I think the biggest thing I bring (to a team) is encouragement…knowing the importance of not only guests, but the staff, so for me, if I can bring in that positive attitude."

— RICH

"I try to bring fun into work. I think it's just inside me; it's who I am. I think when people are having fun at work, they are happier, they are easier to work with, and they're delivering better care to the patients."

— MARY

"That is something that I let people know, that, 'We may be struggling right now, it may be stressful and tense right now, but we're going to be OK. We're all going to make it.'"

— KATIE

"Certainly a positive attitude and that we can find a solution, the ability to think outside the box and find creative solutions."

— CARLA

"What makes her effective?" and "What does he bring to a team?," showing that facilitators create a positive presence

"And she is just absolutely pleasurable to interact with. And she is viewed that way universally. I say very, very pleasant....She brings great energy to every team she engages with....I think she's a bit of a catalyst by bringing her strengths to the team."

— ALICE'S SUPERVISOR

"And the other thing they do is constantly displaying a positive attitude. They both just have a strongly positive presence in any group."

— LYNN AND MARY'S SUPERVISOR

"I would say Susan's not got necessarily an extremely outgoing personality....When she gets involved in something, when she's advocating for something, it's got a positive-looking kind of attitude. She does bring positive energy, positive ideas, into a meeting."

— SUSAN'S SUPERVISOR

"Katie also brings a boundless enthusiasm and a positive attitude that, at the end of the day, really helps...when the going gets rough in a project."

— KATIE'S SUPERVISOR

"He has a positive attitude; he never says anything bad about anyone else. He's optimistic, positive about people....I mean he's just likeable and approachable. He's friendly, he's likeable, a great guy."

— RANDY'S SUPERVISOR

"It could be as simple as starting a meeting with an icebreaker activity, or more she just doesn't take herself too seriously, so she's not afraid to ask questions and poke a little bit of fun at herself, and that makes it fun for others that are there."

— JEAN'S SUPERVISOR

"He's a big energy guy. People love working with him. People just like spending time with him."

— ADAM'S SUPERVISOR

"I think they're both fun to hang around with. I think that's something that other people recognize, too. When you work with them, you recognize they're fun to work with. They keep things a little bit light."

— ELLEN AND ADAM'S SUPERVISOR

"She is a very upbeat, positive, easy-to-get-along-with person....I think they (coworkers) would say she's personable."

— CARLA'S SUPERVISOR

"I think her overwhelming kindness would be something that everyone would see."

— SANDY'S SUPERVISOR

"With his high energy and his...work ethic of, 'Come on guys, we have a job to do. Let's take care of each other. We're letting this negativity get to us and we're picking at each other'...He's the energy guy....He's very friendly, very outgoing."

— STEVE'S SUPERVISOR

"Loren loves what she does....And she's so excited to be sharing with people. But it's authentic enthusiasm. And I think it's catching."

— LOREN'S SUPERVISOR

Bringing a positive presence through humor and wit

"I'm also kind of a goofy person, and my teammates know that, so I might say (snapping her fingers), 'We can do this!' or make a funny joke or do a funny dance move sometimes; I just lighten the mood any way I can."

— CHRIS

"Sometimes when I'm in a meeting, I tend to...this is going to sound weird, but I kind of look for opportunities to say a joke, a one-liner or something. I tend to crack little jokes because I feel like this is a hard job for all of us, so I tend to throw in little jokes, a dry sense of humor."

— SANDY

"I think humor can be really helpful to defuse a situation. And sometimes just pointing out the ridiculous things about the situation can be really helpful in alleviating the tension of it. Being able to make light of it in a respectful way can be helpful to just relieve some tension."

— ELLEN

"When there's a tense time, a little bit of lighthearted fun or a joke to make people laugh tends to bring the tone back down. So I think that having fun and being able to laugh with one another is important for being good at your job and being able to do your job well."

— MARY

About facilitators bringing a positive presence through humor and wit

"One other thing I wanted to point out is their sense of humor. They are both people who have great wit and a sense of humor, and I often find myself laughing with them. So they are able to get to the lightness that is hard to get at after a long clinical day. Anyone here would say they have a 'joie de vivre.' They love their lives, and they love a good laugh, and I think that's really important."

— SANDY AND KATIE'S SUPERVISOR

"She is also fun to work with and has a great sense of humor."

— ELLEN'S SUPERVISOR

"I think they would tell you she's humorous. She has a good sense of humor about herself, about situations."

— LOREN'S SUPERVISOR

"He definitely has humor. I wouldn't say he's like a jokester, but he definitely has a sense of humor."

— RICH'S SUPERVISOR

"Claire brings a certain level of humor to the team."

— CLAIRE'S SUPERVISOR

presence" over "positive energy." Energy connotes an outward display of enthusiasm more characteristic of extroverts. While some facilitators describe a more active and direct enthusiasm, many of the facilitators are self-described introverts. For these individuals, supervisor comments painted a picture of a personal demeanor that, although less apparent, exerted a positive influence on others. In those cases, terms and phrases such as *kind, comfortable to be around, supportive*, and *optimistic* were used to describe exemplary facilitators.

Another aspect of positive presence is humor and wit, mentioned by several facilitators and their supervisors. Exemplary facilitators use humor to decrease stress or lighten the burden of difficult work. The humor was described in various forms: telling brief jokes, poking fun at themselves or the situation facing a team, or inserting a witty comment.

What's more, the facilitators' positive presence was evident in my face-to-face meetings with them. My individual interviews with the facilitators were pleasant encounters. Some of the facilitators were a bit nervous, but, without exception, they were friendly, smiled often, and seemed happy to be involved. They were accommodating. If I had technical problems with the recording equipment, they were patient and tried to help. When preparing for the interview, they assisted by arranging chairs. Although they were busy people, I never felt that I was causing an inconvenience. I felt energized after the interviews. I could see why others would enjoy being around them.

For all employees it can be hard to maintain a positive outlook in a demanding work environment. Over time, even an ideal job can become tedious and stressful. The replacement of a supportive boss or friendly coworkers with someone lacking social skills can transform a pleasant work setting into an unpleasant one overnight. To maintain a positive presence, employees can learn new ways to enhance awareness of their emotions, their physical state, and their immediate surroundings. For example, practices to improve self-awareness in the work environment, such as mindfulness,[12] can instill new purpose and satisfaction in one's job. Yet exemplary facilitators don't seem to need to work at positivity, even in stressful times.

In addition, I would like to stress that exemplary facilitators promote a positive work environment not only for themselves but for others. Each supervisor in this study noted that facilitators convey a positive presence when working with teams and coworkers. It was unanimous. This finding challenges the stereotype of a task-focused, detail-oriented "bean counter" who tracks projects but falls short in the interpersonal domain. It also points out a shortcoming of project managers like Carrie and Dawn (p. 17) who have mastered all the change-management tools but are ineffective because they fail to motivate team members to fully engage. Natural facilitators exude optimism, a positive outlook—an inherent personal attribute that they bring to their work environments. Coworkers can't help but notice it, and, based on the interview responses from supervisors, are more likely to engage in team-based efforts because of it.

CHAPTER 7

Remaining Calm
Emotional Self-Management

"She's kind of unflappable," "She just doesn't get rattled," "She doesn't react or get hooked," "He's sort of a calming influence." Those descriptions were common among the supervisors when asked how the facilitators responded to stressful situations. The majority of exemplary facilitators identified "staying calm" as a strength. Some reported an awareness of their internal emotional reactions in work situations, but overt emotional responses were kept in check during interactions with others. According to their interview responses, when others are stressed, facilitators respond with objectivity, inquiry, or taking steps to help. In short, emotional self-management is a personal attribute of all exemplary facilitators.

> "He who acts upon his impulse always has to regret."
>
> SIGN POSTED ON GROUNDS OF WAT CHIANG MAN, A BUDDHIST TEMPLE IN CHIANG MAI, THAILAND[13]

The ability to identify and to manage one's emotions is a core component of emotional intelligence.[14] The ability to self-regulate our emotions enhances our ability to plan and to solve problems. Goleman writes about the emotional "hijacking" that can take place in the brain. Strong emotions, such as anger or anxiety, can overflow and interrupt communication and problem solving. If emotional reactions become a pattern, they can disrupt relationships. Trust

About remaining calm

"I think by nature I am a calm person. I'm not going to get all frazzled and dramatic and feed into other people's stress. Instead, I will acknowledge it, ask about it, 'What's going on?' Sort of try to gauge if they are looking for help or they just want to talk."

— JEAN

"In a crisis moment, I'm very calm and able to work through the situation...de-escalate the situation."

— LOREN

"I think in a meeting when emotions are getting higher, again trying to stay calm and trying to bring people back to what our ultimate goals are...I see my role as remaining calm, and just trying to be as objective as I can about what is going on."

— ELLEN

"To be successful? It's important to stay calm and prioritize your tasks."

— CHRIS

"Calm, even-keel. That's how coworkers would describe me."

— RANDY

"I generally don't get put off by stress....So when people around me in the clinic are being stressed out, that's when I almost think I'm at my best, when I can step in and assist with what they need to get past it, because nobody wants to live in that stressful space very long."

— KATIE

"So I think once I built that trust in that department...they would come in and talk to me, bouncing things off, and they would know I'm not going to overreact. That's another thing, not overreacting. Work the problem, take your time, handle things as they come up."

— STEVE

"What do I bring to a team? I think being able to remain calm; it's important for being on a team."

— MARY

"Like if I look at an email or a request, I do not react. If it's something that is upsetting, I always try to step back from it, re-read it a couple of times to make sure I've understood it. I try very hard not to react."

— LINDA

"One of the things I focus on is remaining calm. I think that's very important in my role as a social worker, but even in my role facilitating a committee. It's important to stay calm."

— LYNN

"As far as team meetings go, I think a really relaxed, deep patience can help the team move forward."

— ADAM

About facilitators remaining calm

"And part of the attribute is that she doesn't react or get hooked by things.... She's remarkably calm. She will intervene if it's getting too escalated. She's pretty good about setting boundaries, and yet she doesn't herself become engaged in a back and forth."

— JEAN'S SUPERVISOR

"I would say the notion of her calm, levelheadedness is a headline for Alice."

— ALICE'S SUPERVISOR

"I think there's very little you could throw Loren's way that would be surprising to her...She's typically super jovial, kind of happy. She's always...level."

— LOREN'S SUPERVISOR

"She is kind of unflappable; it's hard to tell when she's under stress."

— ELLEN'S SUPERVISOR

"They are both really calm and seem to weather any storm with minimal challenge. They are always calm, thoughtful, reflective, and then able to communicate their thoughts respectfully."

— LYNN AND MARY'S SUPERVISOR

"One of the things I've noticed in Linda is she will not get visibly upset. Now I think she does have a side in which she thinks, 'That was not done right,' but I think she's got a lot of self-control."

— LINDA'S SUPERVISOR

"When she's distressed, she's not impulsive. She tends to calculate, is what I've noticed. If there's a stressful situation going on, instead of jumping the gun and impulsively coming to a decision on something, she would sit back and say, 'Let's think about this situation and talk about this.'"

— CARLA'S SUPERVISOR

"I mean Randy is almost unflappable. He doesn't get stressed. Everybody else can get wound up, but he's sort of a calming influence. He's not purely analytical, so it's not like he's detached, but it's not the other extreme. Yeah, that's a big strength, his calm demeanor."

— RANDY'S SUPERVISOR

"How does he respond to stressful situations? He kind of brushes it off.... He doesn't let others bother his emotions much."

— RICH'S SUPERVISOR

is eroded. People become avoidant or withhold their opinions from others for fear of eliciting an emotional overreaction.

In the workplace, emotional self-management has been linked to success at skills such as coping with frustration and stress as well as maintaining interpersonal relationships. For some, we can see the roots of this in childhood. The ability to control impulses and delay gratification at an early age is associated with increased adaptive behaviors in adulthood, including the facilitator's ability to remain organized and to think ahead and plan more effectively when under stress. Indeed, emotional self-control is called the "master aptitude" underlying emotional intelligence.[14] It is not surprising, then, that most of the exemplary facilitators in this study are described as excelling in emotional self-management.

While facilitators are good at remaining calm, they're not always perfect. Three of the facilitators mentioned emotional self-control as an area for further improvement. They describe being aware of their own internal emotional reactions, such as frustration or impatience, in their work environment. Although they deny expressing strong emotions in the presence of customers or coworkers, they sometimes vent their feelings elsewhere, such as in the presence of a trusted colleague, friend, or their supervisor. They also note that self-control of their emotions has improved compared to earlier in their work career.

CHAPTER 8

Genuinely Caring
Commitment to Helping Others and the Organization

The facilitators care—a lot—about their coworkers, customers, and the organization. They derive satisfaction from helping others. They are passionate about what they do. And they believe in the mission of the organization. This characteristic, caring, is not unique to exemplary facilitators. However, because it was described universally by the exemplary facilitators and their supervisors, it warrants inclusion in the list of personal attributes.

"People who care about each other enjoy doing things for one another. They don't consider it servitude."

ANN LANDERS

Caring was described in several ways. Most commonly it was mentioned as general caring and compassion for others and the job itself, such as "They are passionate about what they do," "I really like helping," or "I love this job." And there was depth to the description. It wasn't a lukewarm, tepid degree of caring; it was described with enthusiasm and certainty. The majority of participants had worked for their organization for many years. They were very familiar with their coworkers and customers. Some expressed a sense of loyalty and commitment to the group and their mission.

About caring and compassion

"For me, if you're working from that deep seat of compassion for others, then you'll help them get there, help the rest of the team get there, help your learners get there."

— ADAM

"I'm passionate about my work. What really gets me excited is when I see managers and our employees embodying the guidance or lessons or practices I believe are best for the organization."

— LOREN

"So I love bringing people together and encouraging them to solve problems. I want everyone here to love their job as much as I do."

— JEAN

"You've got to be a people person. You've got to have a servant's heart....You need someone there who can relate to people. So that's really my function."

— RICH

"I love, I mean love, facilitating."

— ALICE

"I really like to see that people get excited about making a difference for patients and their health and well-being...getting satisfaction out of their success. Yes, that is very satisfying to me."

— KATIE

"What brings satisfaction? People's success; that makes me happy....
But I'll also get these cards or candy, and things like that, for them
(coworkers). Kind of getting them out when they're down in the dumps."

— CLAIRE

*"I love working with patients; I like it when
patients come back, I've been here twenty
years, when patients come back and they've
made some great changes in their life. I
also love the collaboration we have here at
the clinic and the ability to work as a team
together."*

— LYNN

*"'What can I do to
help you, man?' That
really is what it is.
'How can I help you
be successful?' That
was my little saying
out there in the plant,
because it really is,
'How can I help you be
successful?'"*

— STEVE

"I like working with groups. And I feel like I
have good working relationships with all of
our staff here. So that makes me happy too,
getting to work with good people."

— MARY

About the caring and compassion of facilitators

"She genuinely values people...and their well-being at work and ensuring they're being treated right....I see it being an advocate for others. Having interests that go beyond her personal interests....It's part of her concern for others."

— LINDA'S SUPERVISOR

"Claire is someone who, first and foremost, genuinely cares. I mean, that's the start of it... some level of internal knowledge of, 'Hey, I made a difference.' 'Is this person's life better?' 'Is this person's job easier?' I think those are the biggest cup-fillers for her."

— CLAIRE'S SUPERVISOR

" They are both intelligent individuals who care a lot about colleagues, they care about their patient....For each of them, the idea of making a difference in people's lives. That's true for a lot of us, but it's especially true for them."

— ELLEN AND ADAM'S SUPERVISOR

"She (Sandy) also is a very caring and intelligent individual. She is very kind and caring and quite bold in her caring in a very positive way. Katie (displays) some of those same things. This seems to be the thing that makes both of these women tick—devotion to making this clinical place a better place."

— SANDY AND KATIE'S SUPERVISOR

"Success of others and success of the program…it's not focused on herself, it's focused on others, and without question her major source of satisfaction is seeing others be successful."

— SUSAN'S SUPERVISOR

"I think they both really enjoy helping other people, whether that's patients or coworkers. Both of them get great satisfaction from providing help and support."

— MARY AND LYNN'S SUPERVISOR

"Back to that servant leader thing, 'How can I help you? What do you need? How can we both get value out of this?' And when they rise to the challenge and succeed, I think that really makes him feel good."

— STEVE'S SUPERVISOR

"I just think she enjoys working with people. She enjoys the networking with people. And I think she just likes to see things come to fruition."

— CARLA'S SUPERVISOR

"So I think when Loren thinks she can add value, I think that brings her a lot of personal satisfaction….She's not a 'me' person."

— LOREN'S SUPERVISOR

About helping coworkers

"*When others are stressed? If we're short-staffed, I ask what I can do to help, but also, if I see an exam room that's empty. Even though it's not in my job duties, it's helping with the work flow, and it's helping that nurse who's really stressed. So a lot of it is 'doing,' stepping in to ask what I can do to help and noticing what I can do to help even if it's not in my normal role.*"

— LYNN

"If they're shorthanded, I have no problem picking up a soap brush and cleaning a car; being a little more adaptable in that way."

— CLAIRE

"And sometimes in a stressful situation I'll volunteer to do the worst job, or what is considered the most stressful work."

— ADAM

"I always try to be aware that these are not people who say 'no' very often, so I have to be careful about the things I ask them to do because they are much more apt to say 'yes' than to say 'no.'"

— KATIE AND SANDY'S SUPERVISOR

"And when he's asked to fill in for a shuttle or anything else, it's always a 'yes,' and he doesn't complain."

— RICH'S SUPERVISOR

About humility

"And then not really looking for recognition. It really is a lot of the time you're playing the middle man, you're helping facilitate getting things done, but it's somebody else's project that you're helping them to build."

— RANDY

"I want to empower the entire team so that we're all pulling together in the same direction. So I'm committed to shared leadership...how to get people who are shy or untrained in leadership to get more involved. Yeah, I'm not the hero; I try to avoid that."

— ADAM

About the humility of facilitators

"She tends not to focus things toward herself, she tends to deflect it away....She's not a self-promoter. But she takes satisfaction from a job well done. And from seeing others be successful."

— LINDA'S SUPERVISOR

"She is truly a behind-the-scenes person. She doesn't want to highlight herself. She will consistently promote others and help others to be successful....She doesn't like to focus attention on herself....Very selfless in how she gives."

— SUSAN'S SUPERVISOR

"(When) something is going to be completed...he doesn't need to wave a flag and say, 'Follow me.'"

— RANDY'S SUPERVISOR

A brief story shared by his supervisor provides insight into Randy's values. The supervisor stated that Randy likes public service. He went on to explain that several years ago, Randy, who works for the county, left his government job to become general manager for a successful local contractor. But he returned to his current job after a year. I asked why he came back. The supervisor surmised that Randy did not like the "profit-driven side" of private industry; he "did not find the same level of job fulfillment because there wasn't a public benefit." This sense of loyalty and service to others, whether in private businesses or public-service jobs, was a common theme in the interviews.

In some cases, caring is displayed through service to others in the immediate work environment—stepping in to help when needed. When coworkers are stressed or short-handed, facilitators voluntarily step in to help. They willingly complete menial chores or other tasks outside their job description—whatever is needed to support others.

Another dimension of caring that emerged during the interviews is humility. Facilitators described a sense of satisfaction from helping others to succeed. They are comfortable in a supportive role. Several supervisors emphasized that facilitators prefer to avoid attention for their work. They are gratified to see the group succeed and don't desire to receive personal credit. Several interviewees gave a similar message; they are uncomfortable in the limelight and prefer to deflect the credit to the group.

Caring, in a work environment, is based on a personal commitment to coworkers, customers, and the mission of the organization. Employment, for these individuals, is more than a means to a paycheck. It goes beyond an intellectual understanding of the purpose of the organization. These individuals find a deeper level of meaning and satisfaction from their work. They show a high level of dedication and commitment. They form relationships. They stick around. They help. They find their work deeply satisfying.

CHAPTER 9

Offering Systems Awareness
Seeing Around Silos and Across Boundaries

Jean works in a government office. Her supervisor identified Jean as an exemplary facilitator. Here are some excerpts of my interview with Jean.

KM: "What is needed to be effective in your job?"

JEAN: "I think you really do need to understand the organization as a whole before you can be super effective. So that's organization-wide, when I talk about connecting the dots, because there's a lot of that. You need to get out of this bubble of a building...doing a lot of listening, observing, and relationship-building both inside the organization and outside the organization."

KM: "Can you say more about that?"

JEAN: "Our organization is made up of smart, passionate people, and they're experts in their field, but that's where they like to be and that's where they hang out, and it's their own little echo chamber. And so in my role I need not to get sucked into any echo chamber but see the context of why a project even came up....I have the benefit of working across the organization before coming into this position."

> "She also has this system-wide view of how things work and how to get things done. She has a wealth of relationships that she can call on to affect things."
>
> SUSAN'S SUPERVISOR

Jean is a rock star of *systems awareness*: understanding and working with the interconnections among different parts of an organization. It can include knowledge of resources in other departments—knowing that Joe Smith has expertise on a certain topic. It is augmented by relationships or work experience with colleagues in other areas of the organization. A systems perspective is understanding that the components of an organization do not exist in isolation, the oft-called "silos." Jean, quoted above, uses the term "echo chambers" to describe how work groups tend to communicate within their department but are uninformed of the interests and activities of other sub-groups within the same organization. Systems awareness acknowledges that the components are connected; that change and process improvement is more effective when people from disparate areas are consulted or directly involved. Systems awareness is demonstrated when forming a taskforce and intentionally selecting people from various parts of the organization, or with differing training backgrounds, to provide a broader base of input into process change.

Systems thinking focuses on how individuals, and subsystems, interact with other components of the system. This perspective can be very beneficial to organizations and has been referred to as the cornerstone of the learning organization.[15] Systems thinkers can think globally while acting locally. Such people consider the potential consequences of decisions on other parts of larger systems.

At first glance, it may seem counterintuitive that exemplary facilitators, who naturally focus on tasks and processes, would be aware of the broader, interconnecting parts of their work environment. After all, these are the folks who focus on details, dive into projects, initiate action, smooth out processes, and maintain the momentum. These are the people who see the trees, and organize the trees, rather than look at the forest, or the bigger picture.

But an awareness of the connections among the working parts of the organization differs from a focus on the "big-picture" vision of where the organization is going. A systems awareness is very practical. A systems thinker is likely to consider: "If we are going to change this process, how will it affect that other group of people in the next department?" "If we are implementing a new initiative, let's involve someone from a department who went through this same process last year." "When we are preparing for this special event, let's get broad representation on the planning committee." These are operational questions that connote a systems awareness. They are consistent with the task orientation of natural facilitators. That mindset differs from the "big-picture" leadership discussions or strategic plans about the direction of the organization—how to anticipate the market needs as we move ahead, hiring the right workforce, and related broad questions.

The interview data suggest several reasons why some facilitators are aware of the interconnecting parts of their work environment. Many facilitators have been employed in their organization for a long period of time. Jean, quoted above, had the benefit of working in several departments in her organization before moving into her current position. By having broad work experience in the organization, facilitators come to understand the functions of other areas and have formed relationships with colleagues across the organization.

In addition to employment longevity, some facilitators described job duties that take them across departmental boundaries. These are employees hired to implement more traditional facilitation responsibilities, such as process improvement or project management. They are not tied to one department. Often, they are freed from supervising others. They are expected to move among work areas with the goal of seeing the interconnections. Systems awareness is an expectation of their job. They build relationships across the system intentionally in order to be more efficient at getting things done. They can draw on the established relationships as needed to effect change or complete tasks.

Finally, a systems awareness may be related to the highly perceptive nature of these employees. They are sensitive about the feelings and thoughts of others—how an action in one area might affect others, both individually and collectively. In the words of a supervisor, "Alice is highly intuitive, yes, in the situational awareness, a people awareness, and an ecosystem awareness in terms of actions and reactions to things that go down in the various projects and aspects of her job."

Showing systems awareness

"I like to make sure there is good representation on the team of all of the pieces that need to be there. Making sure there isn't a group that is left out, that their contribution is part of the discussion on things. And because I've worked in so many departments here...making sure everybody is represented."

— MARY

"I also have to be able to see the big picture and how different projects and initiatives relate to each other. It's also important for me to be looped in on a significant amount of information. A lot of things cross over, and because of my support role, colleagues come to me with questions regarding situations that they assume I'm aware of."

— LINDA

"I have a really unique perspective because I see how all the various corners of the clinic are operating, but from a higher level...I have that objective point of view from up here, and I can see all the pockets of everything happening down here in the clinic."

— KATIE

"I have worked here for twelve years. I started as a receptionist, then started improving processes, then got a sales license. I think it's because I've worked in so many departments and have been on the service end of things, I'm coming with an understanding of how much time certain things take and also what customers expect from certain departments and from coworkers."

— CLAIRE

"I'm a point of contact for faculty, especially young faculty....I think a lot of what I do is knowing about resources...and then knowing what they want to do in their research and thinking about opportunities I know about externally—other people that they can talk to and collaborate with."

— SUSAN

About the systems awareness of facilitators

"She also has this system-wide view of how things work and how to get things done....She has a wealth of relationships that she can call on to affect things....Again, sort of that systemic view of how things fit together, how things work."

— SUSAN'S SUPERVISOR

"Yes, and some of it is she has some history with the organization. She also has a history with the community. So she just has such great perspective, that it's useful in so many ways....She's able to connect dots....She has the networks, so she knows people and she knows things that are happening. She's able to create synergies that otherwise wouldn't exist....She sees the whole."

— JEAN'S SUPERVISOR

"I think Alice has an acute awareness of her ecosystem. And how the ecosystem is affected and how it impacts others. I think she has an acute awareness of that."

— ALICE'S SUPERVISOR

"And so they have a really amazing ability to bridge that gap that some of us see between ground-level staff and management."

— LYNN AND MARY'S SUPERVISOR

"She works with everyone from the president's office to this department, including staff. So she's really covering the full spectrum of individuals....Her strength is...being able to build political capital. To be able to call on relationships to be able to do her job."

— LINDA'S SUPERVISOR

This final characteristic, systems awareness, was not universal among the facilitators. It was described by just over half (fifty-nine percent) of the facilitators or their supervisors. It was found among those with a personal history of varied work experience within the organization. It was also noted by those whose job duties required them to connect the dots. Dot connectors can be valuable to organizations. They can reduce the likelihood of duplicating efforts down the hallway, match needs in one area with internal resources elsewhere in the organization, assemble a cross-section of coworkers for better process-improvement outcomes, and provide suggestions that maximize assets and expertise.

CHAPTER 10

Final Attributes
Additional Strengths and Family Roots

In this chapter I present additional themes that emerged during the interviews. First are three strengths identified by a minority of facilitators. These strengths did not meet the criterion of characteristics present in at least half of the interviews but are still worthy of mention. I end the chapter with the responses about facilitation traits in the participants' families of origin.

"My mom is the glue of our family. She's the one that brings everyone together. She's the peacemaker, the mediator, and I definitely see a lot of her in me."

KATIE

ADDITIONAL STRENGTHS

Several facilitators identified *reliability* as an important element for their effectiveness. It was mentioned by seven of the facilitators or their supervisors. Related phrases included *follows through*, *dependable*, and *responsive to requests*. The participants linked reliability with building trust among coworkers and customers.

Reliability is not unique to facilitators, but it is another reason why colleagues and customers like working with them. Others come to depend on them. Typically, requests don't languish in their in-box. Because of this trait, they develop a reputation of being the "go-to" person.

Illustrating their reliability

"And, so, building some trust and following through. If people bring you problems and you don't follow through, they'll stop talking to you. If you want them to keep coming, and you can actually improve things, you need to be able to follow through."

— SUSAN

"I would say that coworkers would say I'm very reliable. They know they can absolutely know that I'll follow through."

— SANDY

"I think part of the relationship building...is being respectful, being responsive, providing clear directions, these types of things. There are people who are incredibly easy to work with. They acknowledge every email you send them. They are very clear. Those are people I enjoy working with. They're easy to work with. And I hope that's how people feel about me."

— LINDA

"So if a supervisor asked me if it got done, it did. He knew that it was done. And that made me feel good that he trusted me to know that if I told him it was done, it was done."

— STEVE

Highlighting the reliability of facilitators

"Just some of the basics, why she's a great employee. She always follows through. She always does what she says she is going to do. So I think that honoring commitments to people is what gives her so much credibility."

— JEAN'S SUPERVISOR

"She's authentic. I think that's really important, that if you believe what you're saying, people can feel that. They sense when you're genuine. Loren is a person who sticks to her word."

— LOREN'S SUPERVISOR

"She has a reputation...if Alice says she is going to do something, or if somebody asks Alice to take care of something, there is no doubt it is going to get done. And it's going to get done in a very high-quality way. So her tenacity and commitment to follow-up are absolutely stellar."

— ALICE'S SUPERVISOR

Flexibility is another personal attribute mentioned in several of the interviews. Four interviewees and one supervisor described the need to be *adaptable to constant change* and be *willing to compromise* to resolve issues.

An additional characteristic, *relationship-building,* was described in four interviews. While all facilitators were described to interact easily with co-workers and customers, some interviewees specifically mentioned the ability to *develop relationships.* Building new relationships was linked to the ability to establish trust and to "get things done" more efficiently, especially across departments in the broader organization.

FACILITATION AND THE FAMILY OF ORIGIN

Toward the end of each interview, I asked facilitators about their family of origin. "Now that you have identified the characteristics that make you effective in your job, do you see anyone in your family of origin that has similar characteristics?" The goal of the question was to gain insight into whether the characteristics of exemplary facilitators might be passed down from one generation to the next, as I believe they were in my own family, from my mother to me.

Not surprisingly, the majority of facilitators named one or both parents. A mother or father, or both, were mentioned by fifteen of the seventeen facilitators. The family member most commonly identified as exhibiting facilitation skills was the mother (thirteen of seventeen facilitators.) Nine of the seventeen facilitators identified their fathers as having facilitation characteristics. One facilitator identified his sister as his inspiration for having compassion for others in the work environment. A strong commitment and willingness to work hard was the most common characteristic attributed to fathers and, in two cases, to grandparents. Mothers, on the other hand, were more often linked to caring, support, and organization, in addition to a strong commitment to work.

Mothers modeled facilitation more often than fathers, based on the interview results. Of the thirteen female facilitators, eleven identified at least one facilitation skill in their mother, and five identified at least one facilitation skill in their father. Among the four male facilitators, the most common

Focusing on flexibility

"I like to move with agility. I like to shift gears as the environment dictates."

— LOREN

"Being flexible. There are lots of interruptions in this kind of work....You have to be... comfortable that change is going to happen. The minute you get something figured out, it is going to change."

— CARLA

"Ease of use in being...a little more adaptable in that way....I've been able to jump into roles."

— CLAIRE

"I think a lot of it is flexibility. There's no right or wrong answer to a lot of what we do. It's a lot of flexibility and compromise."

— RANDY

About facilitator flexibility

"If there's a small thing here and there that needs to be done, Claire is very often the one who is able to help me out with it...fill in the cracks, so to speak."

— CLAIRE'S SUPERVISOR

Related to relationship-building

"I'm good at relationship-building. So, I think it's really important in this office to have effective relationships with all the departments, with my colleagues."

— LINDA

"I build rapport and relationships with people relatively quickly."

— KATIE

"If someone new was being hired (for this position), a key characteristic would be relationship-building."

— JEAN

About the relationship-building strengths of a facilitator

"A key component is her ability to develop relationships; really good people skills."

— LINDA'S SUPERVISOR

trait attributed to their parents was a commitment to work hard. Perhaps the results reflect the traditional gender roles in our society. In these families, the mothers exhibited more interpersonal facilitation characteristics, such as caretaking behaviors and support, compared to fathers. With such a small sample size, it is risky to draw any firm conclusions. But it raises the interesting question about whether facilitation behaviors in work environments are more common among females and are an extension of the stereotypical role of mothers in families. It's a question for further research and pondering.

Specific characteristics attributed to the mothers and fathers are shown below (some participants mentioned more than one characteristic):

Mothers' characteristics:	Frequency
Caring for others/helping	5
Positive presence (encouraging, kind, positive, fun)	4
Commitment to work/work ethic	4
Organized/task-oriented	3
Making things smoother (peacemaker, mediator)	2

Fathers' characteristics:	Frequency
Commitment to work/work ethic	4
Caring for others/helping	2
Task-oriented (logical approach to problem solving)	2
Organized/multitasking	1
Positive presence (lighthearted, humor)	1
Making things smoother (talking tactfully)	1

So what conclusions can be drawn from these findings about the family of origin? Most exemplary facilitators grew up around a parent or two who role-modeled some aspects of facilitation. The most common characteristics they

About having characteristics similar to someone in their family of origin

"My mom is the glue of our family. She's the one that brings everyone together. She's the peacemaker, the mediator, and I definitely see a lot of her in me, in those skills that I have learned from her. She will make it a point to make sure we see there are many sides to areas of conflict. I would say she is also just incredibly kind, and she wants people to feel 'everything will be OK.'"

— KATIE

"My mother. She was an amazing person. My mother was so organized. And she was so caring, and loving, and non-judgmental. I think I got those qualities from her. One of the things she said to me that still helps me, she would say, 'Don't worry, honey, it will all work out.' She was very calm."

— SANDY

"My role model is definitely my father. He had an amazing gift, he still does, of making my brother and I feel that we were the most important people to him. He just had the sense to make everyone feel important and worthy. He was able to multitask with the best of them. Even my list-keeping is something I got from my father as well."

— LYNN

"Probably my mom mainly. Helping people. In her daycare she had parents, and she would cook breakfast for their kids...or Halloween and she would make sure they had costumes. Even in our church...when someone needed help or lost a loved one, she cooked meals. So those things that really matter and most people don't think of."

— CLAIRE

"My mother was in teaching for her entire career. She did a really wonderful job of having empathy for all of her students. And she would talk about how important it was to find something to love about everyone she worked with....That's really something that has been helpful to me, both in patient care and in my teaching."

— ELLEN

"For sure my mom is a worker bee as well. In her own role...our family functions...like a well-oiled machine. Because that's just her personality. So I definitely look up to her for that. I think my dad, being an engineer side of him, is very thoughtful and methodical... all the charts."

— ALICE

"My mom and dad. They were both raised on farms, had very strong work ethics. I think as much of anything it's that sense of accomplishment, to be able to complete a task. So I think that's where I got a lot of that, from both of them."

— RANDY

"That isn't hard—definitely my mom. She's somebody who just doesn't give up. She's an encourager. (For) all my plans, she was always an encourager; 'you can do it.' She got her master's and doctorate while raising three kids, and with a smile. She was a pretty amazing lady."

— CARLA

"My dad has always been my work role model. I have a very 'stick-with-it' attitude that I got from my dad. He was very dedicated to his team that he worked with. The lightheartedness, the fun, and the energy I got from my mom. She was the PTA president and the classroom mom. She was in charge of every fundraiser, every bake sale. I inherited the hard working from my dad, and the fun and taking care of people from my mom."

— MARY

observed were a commitment to work, caring for others, a positive presence, being organized and task-oriented, and helping interactions go smoother through mediation and tactful communication. Whether these are inherited traits, learned by observation in the home environment, or a combination of both, they became part of who the facilitators are in their adult lives.

WHAT'S NEXT

Part Three addresses several important questions about exemplary facilitators. They have many strengths, but what are their vulnerabilities? How do they differ from leaders and managers? Can exemplary facilitators move into management and leadership roles? And how can the strengths of facilitators improve the abilities of managers and leaders?

IMPORTANT POINTS FROM PART TWO

In Part Two, I describe seven characteristics of natural facilitators. Here's a summary of important points:

- **Completing Tasks:** A core characteristics of exemplary facilitators is taking action to complete tasks. Rather than create goals or manage personnel, facilitators prefer to work on specified problems or projects. They are adept at working with other individuals and groups to move toward a common goal.

- **Being Organized:** Organization and attention to details is another strength of exemplary facilitators. They keep track of tasks and projects using lists and schedules. They anticipate needs and are constantly looking ahead and preparing for the next steps.

- **Being Perceptive:** Facilitators are able to absorb the social environment. They pick up on subtle social cues by "reading the room"; they actively probe for understanding. Some have a unique talent for listening to varied input, efficiently organizing the content into themes or categories, and keeping a group moving forward.

- **Having a Positive Presence:** Terms used to describe exemplary facilitators include can-do attitude, pleasant, comfortable, friendly, kind, upbeat, energetic, humorous, and fun. People enjoy working with them. They are pleasant to be around. They acknowledge and appreciate others; they infuse a sense of optimism into a group or team.

- **Remaining Calm:** Exemplary facilitators manage their emotional responses. When others are stressed, facilitators respond with objectivity, inquiry, or taking steps to help others. Emotional self-control is a foundation for successful long-term relationships, engenders trust in relationships, and enables objective problem solving.

- **Genuinely Caring:** Exemplary facilitators care, a lot, about their coworkers, customers, the organization, and its mission. They are passionate about what they do. Employment is more than a means to a paycheck. These individuals find meaning and satisfaction in their work. They show a high level of dedication and commitment.

- **Offering Systems Awareness:** Exemplary facilitators are aware of the interconnections within organizations. They understand that the components of an organization do not exist in isolated "silos" but are connected; that change and process improvement is more effective when people from other areas are consulted or directly involved.

- **Additional Strengths:** Three additional strengths are sometimes characteristic of facilitators: reliability, flexibility, and relationship-building.

- **Family Roots:** Most exemplary facilitators grow up around at least one parent who role-models facilitation, most commonly their mother. Common characteristics observed in their families are caring for others, a positive presence, being organized and task-oriented, and improving interactions through mediation and tactful communication.

PART THREE

The Role of Facilitators

CHAPTER 11

Challenges for Facilitators
Vulnerabilities and Areas for Growth

The exemplary facilitators in this study embody many desirable characteristics that likely help their coworkers and organizations be more successful. They are appreciated by their supervisors. But in certain circumstances, some of their strengths can become vulnerabilities.

> "She is the hardest-working person I have ever interacted with. She works too much, to be frank. She probably works eighty to ninety hours a week, even though this is a three-quarter-time position."
>
> SUSAN'S SUPERVISOR

Because of their effectiveness at accomplishing tasks, combined with a commitment to the organization and satisfaction from seeing others succeed, facilitators may become overloaded with work assignments. Supervisors, over time, may come to depend on a facilitator to complete more and more tasks. Facilitators themselves may volunteer to take on more duties. Consequently, their responsibilities may expand beyond their assigned job description, their work hours may be excessive, and their pay may not be commensurate with their contribution to the organization.

The potential for overwork was mentioned in some interviews, as in the supervisor quote that opens this chapter. Some facilitators stated they work in the evenings and on weekends. They tend to be very willing to work longer hours, especially in a work environment where others make a similar contribution. Due to facilitators' talents and "can-do" attitude, the potential for overwork is real and warrants attention. What's more, facilitators may not have the authority or confidence to speak up when they are overburdened. The power differential between a facilitator and supervisor may further impede a resolution to this potential problem. Supervisors and facilitators alike must remain cognizant of the potential of overwork. Facilitators and their supervisors should discuss the topic regularly to ensure clarity of expectations, limits to work hours, and fair reimbursement.

Another potential pitfall for facilitators and the organizations that rely on them is unhealthy enabling. With their proclivity to focus on processes and tasks, and to help others succeed, facilitators may unwittingly enable unwise or unethical business decisions being made higher up in the organization. Several participants emphasized their dislike of participating in strategic planning, "big-picture" discussions. They prefer to place their energy into action, transforming plans into practical application. Yet by focusing on the details, they may overlook the quality of the big decisions. They may assume the direction selected by others is for the benefit of the organization. Being good team players who exude a positive presence, they are at risk to loyally implement a poorly conceived strategy. Although facilitators have many strengths, critiquing the decisions of leaders is not one of them. Nor do they typically assert their opinions to influence the direction of the group. Moreover, some facilitators describe themselves as "people pleasers" who have difficulty speaking out and challenging authority. This problematic scenario has parallels in family life in which one spouse "enables" unhealthy behavior, such as alcohol abuse, by their partner. By keeping the home life as organized and smooth as possible, rather than challenging the partner's behavior, the facilitator enables continuation of unhealthy behavior. In work settings, this potential of enabling unwise decisions or behavior by others in positions of authority is also a vulnerability. To address it, facilitators need to periodically participate in system conversations about the overall direction of the organization and develop skills to assertively express their misgivings when appropriate.

Finally and relatedly, facilitators may find it challenging to stand up to those in positions of power in the work environment. Their natural tendency is to care for others, help when needed, and see others succeed. They are more likely to seek to understand by observing, listening, and inquiring rather than asserting their viewpoints to influence others. When others display aggressive, authoritarian, or abusive behavior, facilitators may avoid dealing with it. And when dealing with it is unavoidable, they may become quite anxious and stressed. This is an area of growth for facilitators. They will benefit from training programs or discussions with trusted colleagues to develop assertiveness skills. Natural facilitators who are promoted into management and leadership positions will likely need to develop their advocacy skills and manage the internalized anxiety generated by confrontation and dealing with power plays in the work setting.

What about those facilitators who express interest in "moving up" in the organization? Can natural facilitators become effective in leadership and manager roles? Yes, but they may face some developmental challenges. When required to, facilitators are able to expand their behavioral repertoire to move into leadership and management positions. Many of their personal attributes, such as positive presence, empathy, and compassion, fit well with the responsibilities of leaders and managers. However, their satisfaction and effectiveness may be impeded by some of their other natural tendencies. For example, in a leadership role, they may be hampered by their focus on task completion and attention to detail. The focus on the trees rather than the forest may result in micromanagement or spending excessive time with detail rather than the larger picture. Similarly, being highly sensitive to others' feelings, including a desire to please others, can impair decision-making. One study participant, recently hired in a middle-management role, reported suffering from "anticipatory anxiety" when faced with difficult personnel decisions. Although she reports her skill improved over time, she still dreads difficult conversations.

In short, exemplary facilitators who move into leadership or management positions will benefit from training as well as professional coaching, mentoring, and/or periodic discussions with trusted colleagues to avoid slipping back into instinctive patterns, such as micromanagement or conflict avoidance. Recommendations for skills development are provided in the next chapter.

CHAPTER 12

Leaders, Managers, and Facilitators
Different Roles Require Different Strengths

Leadership in the Civil War was provided by Generals Grant and Lee, who, along with many other high-ranking officers, developed strategy, communicated the strategy, and inspired others, ensuring that the mission was clear and meaningful. Management was provided by lower-level officers and sergeants. Their focus was on preparing the soldiers through training and discipline. Their role was not to develop strategy but to carry it out.

> "The true measure of leadership is influence— nothing more, nothing less."
>
> JOHN MAXWELL

What about facilitators in this scenario? In the Civil War, an important organizational role for facilitators was in the quartermaster corps. Like the character Radar in the beloved 1970s TV series *M*A*S*H*, they were responsible for keeping track of the inventory and providing the supplies and materials to support the war effort. They organized a system to order, transport, and distribute the food, clothing, equipment, and other supplies. Books about the Civil War typically focus on strategic successes or failures of the leaders and the remarkable, inspirational bravery and suffering of the frontline unit leaders and soldiers. Little is said of the quartermaster role. It occurred behind the scenes. It lacked the glory or excitement of leadership and management. Some might view the quartermaster function as boring and tedious. Yet this supportive role was vital for the success of the overall effort. To Grant's credit as a leader, he recognized that having a well-equipped and well-fed army improved morale and played an important role in the Union's success. He attributed the efficiency of the supply line to his quartermaster corps leader, General Ingalls, who "could move and feed a hundred thousand men without ruffling his temper."[16]

This chapter is about the differences among facilitators, leaders, and managers. After reviewing the attributes of natural facilitators in the previous chapters and considering the three roles in the Civil War, I hope you are beginning to see how facilitators are intrinsically different from leaders and managers. To dive deeper into this distinction, in this chapter I'll comment on role similarities, describe the differences in more detail, and end with suggestions for skills development.

Effective facilitators, leaders, and managers share several characteristics. All three are more successful when they build relationships, take an interest in people, listen well, support teamwork, and offer a systems awareness. Additional role similarities are listed in Figure 1 on page 126.

Let's take a closer look at the characteristics of leaders and managers. This brief review will further distinguish their roles from facilitators and set the stage for the cross-training discussion to follow.

LEADERSHIP

According to the popular books by James Kouzes and Barry Posner, and John Kotter, successful leaders create and communicate a vision, align and inspire people to follow that vision, get the right people on board, and enable others to act.[17] This includes providing and managing financial resources. Jim Collins, in his study of successful organizations, found the leaders of top corporations exhibit a paradoxical blend of personal humility and a fierce resolve to do whatever is needed to make the company great. They are driven, infected with "an incurable need" to produce results.

John Maxwell writes that leadership boils down to one common element:

influencing others.[18] The true measure of leadership is influence. He outlines steps for managers who strive to become leaders: think longer-term, see the larger context, push boundaries rather than enforce the rules, and become agents of change and innovation.

The method of influence can vary, depending on the personal strengths of the leader. Leaders can influence through role-modeling, a servant orientation, inspirational talks, or charisma. Regardless of the method, the common goal is to influence others both within and outside the organization. In a similar vein, Goleman, when writing about emotional intelligence, defines leadership not as domination but as the art of persuading people to work toward a common goal.

Addressing a different target audience of leaders, Bonem and Patterson focus on people in "second chair" positions.[19] This group includes secondary leaders—those in a subordinate leadership role. Citing Maxwell's maxim that leadership is influence, they state the key to leading from a subordinate role is identifying and understanding opportunities to cultivate influence, mainly through strong relationships.

Implicit in the ability to influence others is advocacy. Advocacy, as discussed in chapter 5, is the ability to present a perspective or viewpoint to influence others. Leaders represent the organization to outside constituents. Also, they inspire and align those within the organization. To complete these core responsibilities, leaders must create a compelling vision and, when necessary, provide a clear rationale for decisions. Communicating this information to others, both within and outside the organization, is advocacy in action. Successful leaders must be able to advocate skillfully.

MANAGEMENT

In contrast to leaders, managers provide structure to implement and enforce the organizational mission. This structure includes hiring, training, and supervising people, managing day-to-day operations, communicating standards, and holding staff accountable. Managers often rely on rules and regulations to be certain processes stay on track. Holding people accountable requires assertiveness and, at times, the willingness to make difficult personnel decisions and manage conflict. Those who manage personnel effectively require a balance of relationship skills combined with sufficiently "thick skin" to enforce regulations and, when necessary for accountability, make decisions that may be unpopular and result in negative emotional responses.

Many leadership books, such as those cited above, compare and contrast the roles and requirements of leaders and managers. Both are viewed as vital for the success of an organization.

FIGURE 1: Attributes of Effective Leaders, Managers, and Facilitators

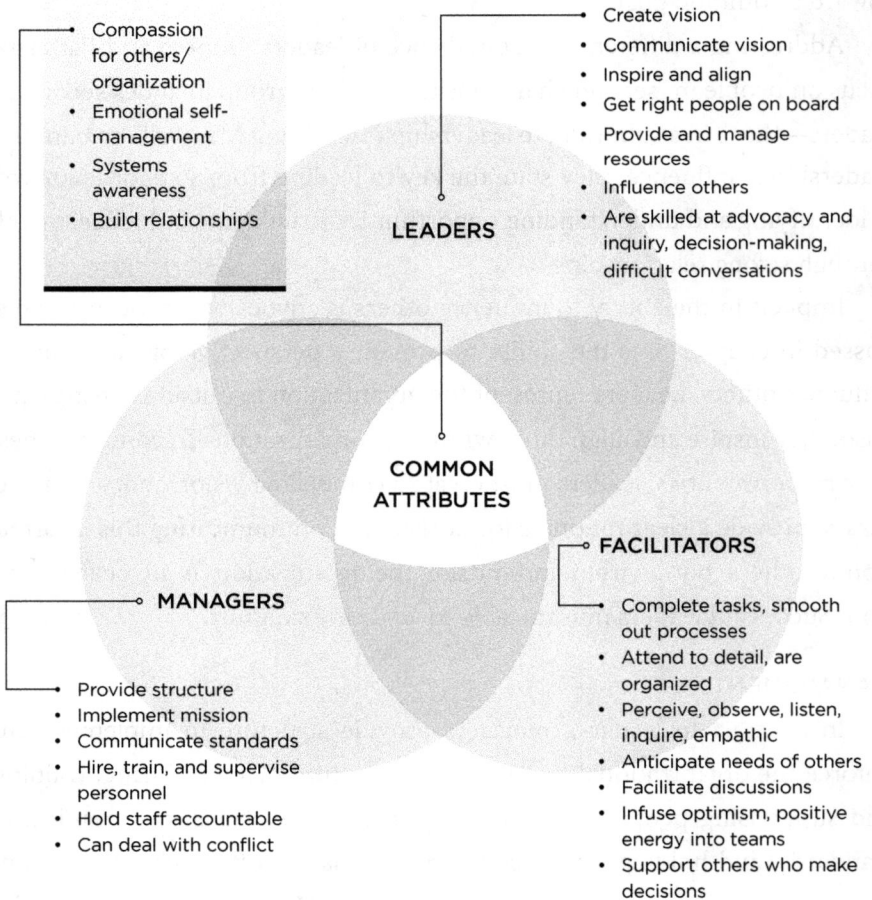

Compassion for others/ organization
• Emotional self-management
• Systems awareness
• Build relationships

Create vision
• Communicate vision
• Inspire and align
• Get right people on board
• Provide and manage resources
• Influence others
• Are skilled at advocacy and inquiry, decision-making, difficult conversations

LEADERS

COMMON ATTRIBUTES

FACILITATORS

MANAGERS

Provide structure
• Implement mission
• Communicate standards
• Hire, train, and supervise personnel
• Hold staff accountable
• Can deal with conflict

Complete tasks, smooth out processes
• Attend to detail, are organized
• Perceive, observe, listen, inquire, empathic
• Anticipate needs of others
• Facilitate discussions
• Infuse optimism, positive energy into teams
• Support others who make decisions

FACILITATOR VIEWS ABOUT LEADERSHIP AND MANAGEMENT ROLES

During the interviews with exemplary facilitators, few of the specific leader and manager characteristics described above were mentioned. The majority of facilitators stated they wish to avoid formal leadership and management responsibilities. They did not express a desire to directly influence others, a key component of leadership. Their influence, when mentioned, was through organization, helping others solve problems, smoothing out processes, and working well together to improve the organizational culture.

In response to the query, "Do you aspire to be in a leadership role?," the majority of facilitators said no or shared ambivalent feelings. They expressed a variety of reasons for avoiding formal leadership and management roles. Several did not wish to supervise others. They preferred to be at the same level as colleagues. Discipline of others, they said, would create feelings of anxiety, guilt, and self-consciousness. They feared a relational gap would develop with their peers.

A few facilitators also expressed anxiety about speaking in front of groups. Several stated openly that they dislike meetings that focus on policy or long-term planning. Many expressed disinterest in discussions about organizational strategy. They preferred that someone else deal with the big picture, threats and opportunities for the organization, decision-making, and the power, finances, and "politics" faced by leaders and managers.

In fact, two facilitators in the study had been in formal leadership positions but intentionally "demoted" themselves in order to be more focused on projects and process improvement. They found the demands of management and leadership to be emotionally draining and less satisfying than a facilitator role. Rather, they gained satisfaction from working with groups on specific projects, willingly organizing timelines and details, finding ways to solve practical problems, and seeing others succeed and taking pride in group accomplishments.

Some facilitators cited the flexibility in their role as a reason for not moving to a formal leadership or management position. The flexibility allowed them to work on projects and not be drawn into administrative responsibilities.

"Do you aspire to be in a leadership role?"

"I will tell you that I never want to be a manager because I don't think I could discipline anybody. That would be really hard for me. I always feel guilty. It would just be so hard for me....It just never seems to interest me."

— SANDY

"I've never really aspired to get into a leadership role; I like to feel like I'm on equal ground with my coworkers."

— CHRIS

"I don't have the urge to be a...manager. I can do it, I understand why it's needed, but...it's just not my favorite thing. I'm more of a people pleaser."

— CLAIRE

"I don't have direct reports...that's OK with me."

— RICH

"I don't have to deal with the hardships, the petty issues and complaints, that the managers and directors have to deal with. That would be difficult for me because I've worked alongside this group of people for so long, I think it would be very hard to be their supervisor...to reprimand people for things."

— MARY

Reasons for disinterest in a leadership role

"I like what I'm doing at this level; sometimes I feel like the politics are really discouraging. Politics are not my strength. I don't think I've ever want to do that."

— SUSAN

"I feel like you can lead from not a leadership position, and you don't have to go to all the meetings; I can't stand meetings."

— ADAM

"I don't like to become involved in the politics."

— SANDY

"So I'm not a big-picture thinker; we have those and we absolutely need them, so we might have several meetings when we need to talk about big-picture ideas, but I don't find myself effective in that type of team....I prefer to be there at what I see as a productive meeting, where I can take some tasks and move a process forward. 'Here's our big idea; how can we make that happen?'"

— LYNN

Citing the flexibility in their current role

"I kind of like my role here because I'm a little in a hybrid role. I like the flexibility I have, and I have really good relationships with the other leaders in the dealership, so I can talk with them, but I have flexibility in my role so I'm happy with where I'm at."

— CLAIRE

"I love my job, and I love right where I am. I've got the best of a whole lot of worlds, doing what I do. So I'm not motivated by title or money; that's never been what motivates me. I'm in a great position where I have a lot of influence without the title. And I like that."

— JEAN

"I like the level of leadership I have now....It's nice because I feel like I can help accomplish tasks—I'm kind of task-oriented. Even looking at my boss's job, there are a lot of times when he's just going from meeting to meeting, dealing with administrative stuff a lot, there's not a lot of 'I got this done or this done.' I get to manage projects and it's really nice. There is satisfaction that I get from completing projects. If I go higher, I just won't get that."

— RANDY

Showing they value their "informal" leadership role

"I feel like I'm in kind of an informal leadership role here. I do a lot of teaching and training with our staff, but I'm not their direct supervisor. I think I have the best of both worlds, because I can lead by example and hopefully inspire others."

— MARY

"It feels, in my role, I'm already kind of a leader in that area; I feel like we've made some great progress improving processes."

— LYNN

"I think I am now, in a way, because I'm the only one who does that, per se. So I set the tone."

— RICH

Finally, several facilitators stated that they liked having "informal" leadership roles, such as training coworkers or leading by example, without the burden of formal management or leadership responsibilities.

Implicit in all of these facilitator statements are personality characteristics that can make it difficult for them to handle leader and manager responsibilities. For example, being highly sensitive to others' feelings can make decision-making difficult. Wanting to please others or avoid negative emotional responses can lead to decision avoidance. A leader or manager who is highly sensitive can become emotionally distraught over even minor decisions or hesitate to hold others accountable. A second example is being detail-oriented or finding satisfaction by completing concrete tasks. This personal attribute of facilitators can result in micromanagement as a leader. Facilitators placed in a leadership position may retreat from their broader responsibilities and focus on their natural interests—specific tasks and processes that, from a leadership perspective, should be assigned to others. As a third example, a facilitator placed in a leader or manager role can get stuck in the inquiry mode. Facilitators are skilled at listening, gathering input, and organizing the information for presentation to others, such as leaders and boards. They also are adept at facilitating group decision-making. However, advocating to influence others is not a strength of facilitators. As we've reviewed, leaders and managers must influence others, advocate for a position, and make decisions. While inquiry is an important component of decision-making, it is only part of the skill set needed by leaders and managers. The story of my own difficulty advocating to correct a source of employee dissatisfaction, told in the opening paragraphs of this book, is a prime example of a facilitator strength (seeking group consensus) impeding leadership behavior.

The preference to avoid leadership roles, voiced by many facilitators, corresponds to the viewpoint of some organizational experts who argue that facilitators are most effective when they remain in their current role. In the 1980s, Robert Kelly wrote in his classic article "In Praise of Followers"[20] that modern organizations will not succeed without the kind of people who take pride and satisfaction in the role of supporting player, doing the less glorious work without fanfare. He identified five types of followers but focused primarily on *effective followers*, the unusual people similar to the natural facilitators presented in this book. According to Kelly, they choose followership as their primary role. They desire to stay in that role. They serve as team players who take satisfaction in helping further ideas and projects. He advocates that organizations should redefine the roles of leaders and followers, thinking of them as equal but different activities. People in effective follower roles have the social capacity to work well with others and the desire to participate in a team effort to accomplish a greater common purpose. In Kelly's opinion, to be successful, organizations should recognize, develop, and reward both effective leaders and effective followers.

CROSS-TRAINING AMONG FACILITATOR, LEADER, AND MANAGER ROLES

While there are many good reasons for facilitators to remain facilitators, it's possible for facilitators to become leaders or managers. It's also possible for leaders and managers to become better facilitators. Let's take a look.

TEACHING LEADERSHIP SKILLS TO FACILITATORS

Many of the natural facilitators I interviewed told me they didn't want to be managers or leaders. They liked their jobs. They thrived in their current roles. They disliked management and leadership tasks. And, as we've seen, the organizations needed them as facilitators.

But sometimes facilitators may want to move into leadership or management roles. Is it possible for them to become effective managers and leaders? The answer is yes, but only if they themselves are truly interested in making the transition.

Managers, understandably, may seek to promote a facilitator due to their strong performance and loyalty. Yet a key difference between exceptional leaders and exceptional followers is *desire*: the desire to lead versus the desire to participate in a team effort for the accomplishment of some greater common purpose.[21] Pushing a talented but uninterested facilitator into a management or leadership role is a disservice to the organization and the employee. Adding managerial or leadership responsibilities to a facilitator's job may dilute their effectiveness and work satisfaction. Before encouraging a natural facilitator to move up in the organization, it is important to understand their genuine interests and work priorities. Some supervisors that I interviewed, recognizing that facilitators are most effective with minimal leadership and management responsibilities, had taken steps to guard their exemplary facilitators from increased administrative duties.

But exemplary facilitators who do want to move into management and leadership roles should receive training and look to specific leadership styles that build upon their natural facilitation tendencies. Many organizations offer access to leadership development training, internally or through external resources. In smaller organizations, training may occur through informal discussions with existing managers and leaders.

Regardless of the training format, an important first step in leadership training for facilitators is starting with a conceptual framework that underscores the differences and similarities among the roles of facilitating, managing, and leading. The diagram on page 126 can serve this purpose. For training purposes, the characteristics in the diagram can be viewed as strengths. For facilitators, learning leadership competencies is less intimidating and more attainable when presented as skill-building. Adding new strengths to their familiar, existing strengths infuses a sense of optimism into leadership development.

Building on a broad conceptual framework, mental models are the second step in leadership training. They can set the stage for learning specific leadership skills. An example of a mental model is the advocacy-inquiry continuum,[10] initially described in chapter 5. Sometimes called the push-pull or assertiveness-listening continuum, it describes complementary approaches for interacting with others. Skills at both ends of the continuum are useful for leaders. Specific skills are needed to advocate effectively, such as delivering a compelling message that influences the thinking or feelings of others. On the other end of the continuum, other skills are needed to inquire, such as listening without judgment and asking insightful questions to understand another's viewpoint. In any given situation, choosing whether to advocate or inquire depends on the context and the desired outcome. This mental model can be used by leaders, managers, and facilitators alike. Natural facilitators will easily recognize inquiry methods, such as posing thoughtful questions, used to "pull" opinions and ideas from others. At the same time, the mental model will help them see how advocacy skills, such as presenting a compelling presentation, can better prepare them to respectfully "push" to influence others when the situation calls for it.

The third and final step, mastering specific leadership skills, is built upon these mental models. This is the stage when new leaders learn concrete skills. An example of a specific advocacy skill is composing a written message explaining a new policy to employees. When teaching this skill, the leadership instructor might start by explaining to the facilitator that organizational changes, such as new policies, are better received when the "why" for the policy precedes the "what," "how," "when," and other details.[22] That is, the *reason* for the new policy should be clearly stated early in the message, followed by the details, such as who it affects and when it will be implemented. As a learning exercise, examples of well-written and poorly written emails, letters, or public announcements can be reviewed and discussed. In this scenario, a poorly written message is one in which the *why* is not apparent. Then, to complete the tutorial, learners can be asked to apply the new information by composing a letter or email about a new (fictitious) policy, followed by feedback from the instructor or fellow learners.

Decision-making is another specific skill that natural facilitators can learn to prepare for a leadership role. Again, a mental model can be useful. For this topic, learners can read about the four common methods for making decisions: command, consultative, vote, and consensus,[23] including examples of each method. For example, when using the consultative method, the leader systematically solicits input from others (consults), then makes the final decision. Through group discussion, learners can better understand the rationale for each decision-making method, along with advantages and disadvantages of each. To make this topic more concrete, learners can examine several meeting agendas and identify which decision-making method would be most appropriate for items that require a decision. Learners can then practice new decision-making skills by role play. When learning about the decision-making methods, natural facilitators will feel most familiar with the consensus method, in which the leader draws out the opinions of others, seeks common ground, and continues the discussion until full agreement is reached. They will be less comfortable, and require more practice, with leader-centric decision-making methods, which are often appropriate and more efficient in a demanding, fast-paced work environment.

Other practical topics, such as engaging in difficult conversations and long-term planning, also can be taught to facilitators moving into leadership or management positions. Regardless of topic, new learning is more likely to be retained and used appropriately when presented in the context of an overall framework of leadership, management, and facilitation roles and relevant mental models that present new skills as an extension of existing strengths.

Speaking of existing strengths, it's important to note that certain leadership styles are better suited to natural facilitators. I encourage natural facilitators who aspire to be managers and leaders to learn more about servant leadership, relational coordination, and other leadership styles that bridge the role of leader and facilitator.[24] These leadership models emphasize shared decision-making, relationship building, inquiry, empathy, and group facilitation skills—all personal attributes of facilitators. Using these models, facilitators can successfully integrate their natural strengths into their developing leadership style.

TEACHING FACILITATION SKILLS TO LEADERS AND MANAGERS

Successful organizations also can use the information in this book about natural facilitators to improve the abilities of leaders and managers. Many leaders and managers already possess some facilitation skills, but these skills can be further enhanced by providing clear descriptions of facilitation skills, use of mental models, and skill application in a supportive learning environment.

Yet I would note that some natural facilitator strengths are more "teachable" than others. Many attributes of facilitators, such as being highly organized, task-oriented, and sensitive to others, are lifelong traits. Responses about their family of origin, discussed in chapter 10, suggest that natural facilitators inherit or learn facilitation skills at an early age. In his book *Good to Great*, Jim Collins posits that the *right* person for a job has more to do with character traits and innate capabilities than with specific knowledge, background, or skills. In light of these observations, efforts to help leaders and managers develop facilitation characteristics such as a positive presence, humor, task completion, and detail orientation will be challenging. In the words of one supervisor, "I don't think you can teach organizational skills in a course." However, well-planned development sessions can, at minimum, help leaders and managers recognize the value of facilitation skills. As a consequence, leaders can intentionally place natural facilitators on teams or work groups where their presence will add value. In addition, select facilitation skills, such as meeting facilitation, active listening, and emotional self-management, are more "teachable" and can improve the competence of those in leadership and management roles.

As with teaching leadership skills to facilitators, a conceptual framework is a good starting place for cultivating the facilitation skills of leaders and managers. As described in the previous section, the diagram highlighting the roles of leaders, managers, and facilitators (page 126) can be a useful stepping-off point when teaching a new skill. By providing examples of facilitation, leaders and managers will realize they already apply these skills to a degree. And, with any skill-development efforts, focusing on strength-building and mental models can enhance the learning.

A very tangible application of facilitation skills for leaders is conducting a meeting. Meetings are frequent activities for leaders and managers. Most can identify elements of a well-run or poorly run meeting based on their experience. The topic "running effective meetings" can be used to teach at least three facilitation skills: directing traffic, active listening, and emotional self-management. The natural facilitator attributes of *being perceptive* (chapter 5) and *emotional self-management* (chapter 7) are directly related to running an effective meeting.

Directing traffic is a shorthand term for the skills needed to enhance the flow of discussion in a meeting. The ability to direct traffic is improved when a leader integrates the strengths of *being tuned in* and *empathy* described in chapter 5. Directing traffic includes a number of micro-skills such as limiting the air time of talkative members, soliciting input from quiet members, using phrases to keep the discussion moving ("Let's hear from others"), staying on task, and keeping an eye on the clock. Of vital importance is recognizing the difference between *facilitating* a discussion and *participating in* a discussion. A leader's primary responsibility is to facilitate a meeting by directing traffic. This task requires that the leader remain observant of others to assess their level of engagement and emotional reactions, and to balance the opportunities for input. Leaders can improve their meeting facilitation skills by watching role models and receiving feedback from skilled observers. At times, a meeting leader may want or need to step in as a participant, providing information or opinions on a topic. When this happens, leaders can easily lose sight of which role they are in (facilitator or participant) and blend the two roles. The meeting can get off track, and participants can become confused about the leader's role. To keep the two roles distinct, leaders can learn strategies such as assigning someone else to temporarily facilitate the meeting or stating explicitly to meeting participants when they, as the leader, are stepping in and out of the participant role.

Active listening is another facilitation skill that can benefit a leader or manager. This is a form of inquiry in which the listener states, in their own words, what they heard from the speaker. It slows down a conversation, ensures that the speaker feels understood, and is especially helpful when communication is breaking down or emotions are surfacing. The section *seeking to understand* in chapter 5 relates directly to this skill. The micro-skills of active listening include listening while suspending judgment and choosing appropriate words to capture the speaker's message, including emotional content (e.g., "You're frustrated that the vote went against your plan."). This skill requires a leader to listen carefully and not think ahead. It ensures others feel understood and can be instrumental in high-stakes conversations or when group consensus is important. This skill can be improved by observing role models and then practicing active listening in pairs.

A third facilitation characteristic, emotional self-management, discussed in chapter 7, is an attribute common to facilitators but not necessarily leaders and managers. The reflexive expression of anger or repeated avoidance of anxiety-producing interactions can impair relationships with coworkers, decrease trust in leaders and managers, and impede their effectiveness. A leader who habitually exhibits frustration or irritability in meetings can inhibit others from sharing their ideas openly. Excessive anxiety can impede a leader's ability to direct traffic effectively. The micro-skills of emotional self-management include the early recognition of one's own emotions and mastery of skills to control or channel the emotions in a productive manner. A presentation of potential strategies, such as deep breathing and self-talk, can set the stage for productive group discussions on this topic. Reading about mindfulness[12] and emotional intelligence[14] can supplement instruction.

Two mental models can help leaders and managers learn these three facilitation skills. One is the inquiry-advocacy conceptual model described earlier. Using the model as a reference, leaders and managers who view their strength as advocating or "pushing" to influence others may see that inquiry or "pull" methods may be more effective in certain situations, such as when running meetings or when involved in emotional or high-stakes discussions. Emotional intelligence is another useful mental model for teaching facilitation skills. Emotional self-management is a foundational skill of emotional intelligence and is a prerequisite for leadership skills such as successfully engaging in difficult conversations.

Leaders and managers who aspire to improve other facilitation skills, such as empathy and other ways to absorb the social environment, may need to supplement training with coaching. New ways of observing and interacting with others take time. Ongoing support and feedback can help new skills become enduring strengths.

CHAPTER 13

Summing It Up
Final Thoughts About Facilitators

What a pleasure it was to interview these talented people. They expressed a sense of honor to be selected by leaders for the study. They were pleasant, responsive, friendly—all the characteristics one would expect. Their supervisors bragged about them. "The perfect employee," one said. Supervisors didn't want to lose them. Facilitators were described as being wonderful employees, a pleasure to work with; their presence helped teams perform better.

> "Oh, it's like gold! She's made my job, my role, so much easier."
>
> LINDA'S SUPERVISOR

The facilitators in this study are not carbon copies of one another. Some are especially talented at organization. Some excel at infusing optimism into difficult situations. Others shine when leading discussions or process change. But all of them share a common set of attributes. And their unique combination of skills breaks traditional stereotypes. For example, people who champion lists, schedules, and process matrices can be typecast as valuing numbers over group morale. Project managers, in some work settings, have the reputation of being taskmasters who pressure the team, issuing reminders to complete forms and meet deadlines. Yet the natural facilitators in this study combine strengths from the head and the heart. From the head they are practical, organized, and methodical in ensuring concrete progress. But at the same time, from the heart, they lift the spirits of the group, help interactions flow more smoothly, and care deeply about the success of others. They possess a hybrid of skills that fills an important niche in organizations.

Despite these positive characteristics, facilitators are not perfect. They are prone to overwork. Through their loyalty and focus on projects, they may unwittingly support ill-advised organizational goals or unethical practices. Their inclination to observe, perceive, and inquire may leave them poorly equipped for situations when advocacy is needed. In other words, they are not superheroes who can do anything. Facilitators lack certain management and leadership skills. Those who desire to move into management and leadership positions will need to develop new skills to offset these vulnerabilities.

I would also be remiss if I didn't point out the shortcomings of this research. It lacks racial, ethnic, and gender diversity among the participants. Of the seventeen facilitators, there were no people of color. Only four were males. While this was a reflection of the employee composition of the selected organizations, it leaves a gap in our knowledge. Do the facilitator attributes described in this study apply to organizations with a more diverse workforce? That remains to be seen with further research.

As I've shared, this project started with my personal experience as a natural facilitator who ended up in leadership roles. Through this study, I found other natural facilitators, and I carefully delineated their characteristics. A central goal of this book is to make people, especially leaders, aware of the importance of facilitators. I recently read a book about medical advances made in the last two centuries. The author provides brief biographical sketches of a number of celebrated scientists and researchers who made important discoveries. As I read each story, I thought to myself, "Each one must have had a facilitator on their team."

My next-door neighbor, a bright, friendly 80-year-old woman, worked twenty years for one professor at the local university. As a world-renowned expert in microbiology, the professor conducted research, wrote articles, and traveled the world to speak to diverse audiences. She coordinated his schedule, prepared his manuscripts, followed up on correspondence, and organized his work life. Loyal to the end, she retired when he retired. My neighbor is a facilitator. My hunch is that the expert owes his success, in part, to her skills.

As is evident in these stories, I often think about the people who support successful individuals and groups. During the course of this project, I became even more acutely aware of their presence and their unique skills, in organizations and families. My hope is that you, too, by reading this book, have come to appreciate these talented "globs of glue" and their important contributions to successful organizations.

IMPORTANT POINTS FROM PART THREE

Part Three addresses challenges as well as opportunities for natural facilitators. After contrasting the roles of facilitators with those of leaders and managers, I provide suggestions for the professional growth of exemplary facilitators. Training strategies are presented for two audiences: facilitators interested in leadership positions, and leaders and managers interested in improving their facilitation skills. Here are specific highlights:

- Challenges for exemplary facilitators include the potential for overwork and dealing with the politics and people in positions of power in the work environment.

- Successful facilitators, managers, and leaders share common characteristics, such as caring for others, the organization, and its mission; systems awareness; building positive, trusting relationships; and maintaining a positive presence.

- Some characteristics of effective facilitators, managers, and leaders are distinct:
  - Leaders: Create and communicate a vision; influence, inspire, and align people; get the right people on board; provide and manage resources; make decisions; advocate to external constituents; engage in difficult conversations

  - Managers: Implement the mission, provide structure, communicate standards, hold staff accountable, hire and supervise staff, engage in difficult conversations

  - Facilitators: Support tasks and projects; attend to detail; keep projects on track; smooth processes; anticipate needs and plan ahead; facilitate group processes and discussions; infuse positive presence; support others who make decisions

- Many natural facilitators do not aspire to management or leadership roles. In such cases, the organization may benefit when managers and leaders allow facilitators to use their strengths and guard against adding administrative or managerial duties.

- For natural facilitators who want to move into management or leadership roles, training programs should build on existing strengths. Facilitators will benefit by learning about leadership styles, such as servant leadership and relational coordination, that integrate their facilitation skills in the leadership role.

- Leaders and managers can benefit by integrating facilitation strengths into their roles. Specific skills include facilitation of group discussions, active listening, and emotional self-management. These skills can be beneficial for conducting meetings and engaging in difficult conversations.

- For facilitators, managers, and leaders, coaching will help integrate new skills into enduring strengths.

Appendix

DETAILS ABOUT PARTICIPATING ORGANIZATIONS

This appendix provides more details about the organizations that participated in my research project. The organizations are summarized in Table 1, on page 24.

The healthcare organizations I selected are medical clinics associated with family medicine residency programs. These programs are training sites for primary care physicians. They are complex organizations with the dual mission of educating primary care physicians and providing medical care for patients with limited resources. Residency programs are housed in outpatient medical clinics. Five medical clinics were selected for this study—four in urban settings and one in a rural community. Each of the four urban clinics employs sixty to a hundred medical staff. All four programs, located in Colorado, have been in existence for at least forty years. Their success is reflected in their remarkable popularity as training sites. To fill six to ten physician training slots each year, the programs receive hundreds of applications from highly qualified medical students. The rural medical clinic, located in Wisconsin, employs approximately forty staff. It prepares family physicians for small town practices. Established in the early 1990s, it is recognized as one of the longest-running rural training clinics in the country. The program receives approximately one hundred applications for its two positions each year.

Employees from one city and one county government are also included in the study. The city government has approximately 1,600 employees. It was the recent recipient of the Baldrige Award for Performance Excellence. The county department of public works, respected for its successful expansion of services to a quickly growing population, includes engineering and planning services. The department employs 189 staff members.

The private businesses that took part in this study include a car dealership and a multinational food corporation. The car dealership, which employees 160 people, has an excellent community reputation, has been in existence for more than fifty years, and has received multiple awards for business excellence. The food corporation has been in existence for over one hundred years. The food corporation's facilitator selected for this study is from the technology section of the research and development department, which employs approximately fifty people.

The university department involved in this study is nationally known for performance excellence. It has been listed consistently in the top ten engineering departments in the United States in the annual *US News and World Report* rankings. The department employs 560 faculty and staff. It attracts high-quality students for its undergraduate and graduate programs.

The electric utility company included in the study employs 350 people and has been in existence for over forty years. A community-owned cooperative, it has been recognized for progress toward environmentally friendly energy methods. Two utility facilitators were interviewed for this project. Both had recently been promoted to management positions.

Thanks and Appreciation

First I want to thank the natural facilitators and their supervisors who volunteered for this project. They agreed to be interviewed and were willing to self-disclose for no apparent gain for themselves. Despite being contacted out of the blue by a stranger, they made room in their busy schedules for an interview. For the facilitators and supervisors alike, I left each encounter thinking what a privilege it would be to have them as work colleagues.

I also appreciate the input of five special friends and colleagues who were willing to hear my preliminary thoughts about facilitators and read the manuscript. They helped shape my ideas, particularly about the differences and similarities of leaders, managers, and facilitators. For their insights, connections to valuable new resources, and gentle challenges, I am indebted to Austin Bailey, M.D., Larry Mauksch, M.A., and Bill Gunn, Ph.D. All three are gifted facilitators. Austin, my supervisor for more than ten years, is a talented blend of leader and facilitator. Chris Hutchinson, founder and leader of the Trebuchet Group, provided helpful input about the roles of leaders and facilitators. I thank my longtime colleague Kristen Bene, Ph.D., who provided feedback through the lens of her research expertise. As a talented editor in her own right, she provided exceptional suggestions for style, grammar, and readability.

Two professionals were invaluable guides for moving this project into publishable form. Launie Parry of Red Letter Creative designed the cover and laid out the interior of the book. Karla Oceanak is a gifted editor and informal teacher. She tutored me on the finer points of reader engagement and provided the final editing of the manuscript so it spoke with greater clarity and coherence.

Closer to home, I am grateful for two family members who willingly volunteered to edit the transcript. My son, Aron, a grammarian in an age when grammar is not always valued or understood, caught more errors than I care to admit. And my wife, Connie, a retired public schoolteacher, read with an eye for accuracy and sentence structure. In addition to editing, she was a supportive partner, listening patiently as I obsessed about this seemingly endless book project.

Finally, I must come full circle back to my mother, Frances Marvel. Her story as a gifted natural facilitator was told in the introduction. It's appropriate to end the book by again acknowledging her humble, positive presence. She truly made things go more easily for everyone around her.

Endnotes

These notes are intended as a quick guide for those who wish to do further reading on a topic.

1. The story about Shane Battier comes from "The No-Stats All-Star," an article in the *New York Times Magazine* (2009). In this article, writer Michael Lewis provides a great example of a facilitator in a major sport: "When he's on the court, his teammates get better, often a lot better..."
https://mobile.nytimes.com/2009/02/15/magazine/15Battier-t.html
I am indebted to Larry Mauksch for calling my attention to this excellent resource.

2. The pilot study was conducted in 2017 in four urban medical clinics. I interviewed seven employees and three supervisors to better understand the characteristics of natural facilitators in medical environments. Colleague Kristen Bene and I published the results in the September 2019 issue of *Family Medicine*.

3. Definitions of terms in the first chapter came from *The American Heritage College Dictionary, Third Edition*. Boston: Houghton Mifflin Company; 1993.

4. I was surprised to learn that the concept of a human catalyst has been used for decades, if not centuries. More information about the human catalyst as a role in organizations can be found in this link:
http://www.eoht.info/page/Human+catalyst

5. The term "implementation genius" comes from the work of Hans and Annemarie Bleiker. More information about their training model *Systematic Development of Informed Consent* can be found on their website:
http://www.consentbuilding.com

6. There are many professional articles about the skills of external facilitators (trained facilitators who are brought into an organization on a temporary basis). Two articles, cited here, were used for writing this paragraph. The article by Harvey and her colleagues, with their description of a facilitation continuum, is especially valuable.

   Kittson A, Harvey G, McCormack B. "Enabling the Implementation of Evidence-Based Practice: A Conceptual Framework." *Quality in Health Care*, 1998;7(3):149-158.

   Harvey G and colleagues. "Getting Evidence into Practice: The Role and Function of Facilitation." *Journal of Advanced Nursing*, 2002;37(6):577-588.

7. The concept of a "big, hairy, audacious goal" is described in *Good to Great* (2001). According to Jim Collins, a BHAG is a huge goal that is clear and compelling; people "get it" right away. It serves as a unifying focal point that galvanizes people to work together.

8. David Allen's book *Getting Things Done: The Art of Stress-Free Productivity* (2001) is full of practical suggestions for increasing one's personal organization and efficiency. The natural facilitators interviewed for this book could have been the poster children for Allen.

9. In his classic book *Emotional Intelligence: Why It Can Matter More than IQ* (1995), Daniel Goleman describes personal characteristics, such as empathy and self-awareness, that have more to do with success in life than high IQ. Being in tune with others sets the stage for successful interpersonal relationships. Self-awareness is a prerequisite for emotional self-management. Research presented in the book shows a clear link between these characteristics and success in work environments.

10. I have found the advocacy-inquiry dichotomy to be an extremely useful model for understanding basic human interactions. Peter Senge presents the *advocacy-inquiry* concept as a mental model in *The Fifth Discipline: The Art and Practice of the Learning Organization* (1990). Chris Argyris describes a similar conceptual model as *pushing and pulling* in his book *Knowledge for Action: A Guide to Overcoming Barriers to Organizational Change* (1990). In a third similar model, Thomas Gordon describes the *assertiveness* skill and the *listening* skill in his book *Leader Effectiveness Training* (2001). All three of the writers are getting at two basic intentions

when communicating: putting one's own viewpoint out to others (advocacy, pushing, asserting) and obtaining input from others (inquiry, pulling, listening).

11. The study about "pushing" and "pulling" in administrative meetings was conducted in medical settings. The complete results are presented in an article published with my colleagues Kristen Brezinski (now Bene) and Bill Gunn: "Push and Pull: Resolving Differences of Opinion During Meetings" in *The Physician Executive*, Sept/Oct 2004.

12. The practice of mindfulness can be valuable for those who wish to enhance several of the characteristics described in this book, such as absorbing the social environment (chapter 5), remaining calm (chapter 7), and having compassion for one's work (chapter 8). Helpful resources include *How We Work: Live Your Purpose, Reclaim Your Sanity, and Embrace the Daily Grind* (2018) and *Attending: Medicine, Mindfulness, and Humanity* (2017).

13. This sign caught my attention when my wife and I visited an ancient temple in Chaing Mai, Thailand. The phrase was hand-painted and nailed on a tree in the temple courtyard. It was a nice reminder that emotional self-management is valued across cultures and over time.

14. My discussion of emotional self-management is informed by two books. First is *Emotional Intelligence*, described in endnote 9, above. The second book is *The Marshmallow Test: Why Self-Control is the Engine of Success* (2014) by Walter Mischel. The author reviews the extensive research that has evolved from the simple test in which a child is presented a marshmallow and given a choice: eat this one now or wait and enjoy two later. The results link the ability to delay gratification at a young age with success later in life. That's why Mischel labels emotional self-control the "master aptitude."

15. My first exposure to systems thinking was as a clinical psychology trainee. Family therapy is built upon an awareness of the family system: a change in the behavior of one person affects other family members. Change is more effective when the larger system is taken into account and, ideally, directly involved. In *The Fifth Discipline* (1990), also mentioned in endnote 10, Senge applies systems thinking to organizations. He describes the five characteristics of a learning organization: personal mastery, mental models, shared vision, team learning, and systems thinking.

16. The information about Grant and the role of the quartermaster corps, under the direction of General Rufus Ingalls, was obtained from Ron Chernow's *Grant* (2017). Another facilitator in Grant's professional life was Captain John Rawlins. As Grant's loyal personal assistant and chief of staff, he coordinated Grant's internal staff and monitored his personal well-being, including his alcohol use.

17. The characteristics of successful leaders are gleaned from several sources, starting with *The Leadership Challenge* (2007) by James Kouzes and Barry Posner, *Leading Change* (1996) by John Kotter Ph.D., and *Good to Great* (2001) by Jim Collins.

18. John Maxwell, in his book The *360 Degree Leader: Developing Your Influence from Anywhere in the Organization* (2005), emphasizes that *influence* is the essence of leadership.

19. Several authors have written about mid-level leaders—those who lead and influence but are not in the top position of authority. Three examples are *The 360 Degree Leader: Developing Your Influence from Anywhere in the Organization* (2005) by John Maxwell, *Leading from the Second Chair: Serving Your Church, Fulfilling Your Role, and Realizing Your Dreams* (2005) by Mike Bonem and Roger Patterson, and *Getting Things Done When You are Not in Charge* (1993) by Geoffrey Bellman.

20. The article by Robert Kelly, published in *Harvard Business Review* (1988), celebrates the role of effective followers. He encourages organizations to cultivate effective followers as well as effective leaders. "In almost all companies, leadership is taught and encouraged while followership is not; yet effective followership is a prerequisite for organizational success."

21. This key difference between exceptional leaders and followers (the *desire* to lead versus the *desire* to participate in a team effort) is credited to Robert Kelly in his article "In Praise of Followers" (see endnote 20, above).

22. According to Simon Sinek, the "why" is the thing that inspires people. More information about this mental model can be found in his book *Start with Why: How Great Leaders Inspire Everyone to Take Action* (2009) or by watching his TED talk.

23. More information about methods for making decisions can be found in *Crucial Conversations: Tools for Talking When Stakes Are High* (2002) by Kerry Patterson et al.

24. Several leadership models focus on interpersonal relationships, emotional intelligence, and shared decision-making. Examples include servant leadership (*The Power of Servant-Leadership*, 1998, by Robert Greenleaf), emotionally intelligent leaders (*Primal Leadership*, 2002, by Daniel Goleman), relational coordination (*High Performance Healthcare: Using the Power of Relationships to Achieve Quality, Efficiency, and Resilience*, 2009, by Jody Hoffer Gittell), relationship masters (from the Harvard First-Year Outdoor Program Leader Handbook https://harvardfop.github.io/interpersonal-skills/no-doze.html), and relationship-centered administration (*Leading Change in Healthcare*, 2011, edited by Anthony Suchman, David Sluyter, and Penelope Williamson).

About the Author

Kim Marvel, Ph.D., grew up with a natural facilitator (his mother) and a relationship-centered leader (his father). Over the course of his career, he became more aware of both roles in work environments. Dr. Marvel started his career as a college psychology instructor and soon moved into graduate medical education. His roles included teaching, patient care, research, faculty development, organizational development, leadership, and facilitation. He has a Ph.D. in clinical psychology and an M.A. in college teaching of psychology. Prior to retirement, Dr. Marvel served as the Director of the Colorado Association of Family Medicine Residencies and the Colorado Commission on Family Medicine. He lives with his wife, Connie, in Fort Collins, Colorado.